For Jeff, the love of my life and my tower of strength.
For Ella and Maya, the light of our lives, our sun, moon and stars.
Daddy and papa love you very much.

I0123579

In the best interest of the children

A true story

LIEVEN VANDENDRIESSCHE

DESIGN: abeloosdesign
PHOTOGRAPHY: Wannes Vandendriessche

ISBN 978 90 8666 345 3 soft cover
ISBN 978 90 8666 346 0 hard bound
NUR 740

Publisher: Mosae Verbo, Maastricht

Contents

Preface

This book tells the extraordinary story of how we adopted our two beautiful daughters.

It is also the story of a period in Flanders and Belgium (2007-2012) when there was a huge disparity between what the law said and how adoption policy worked in practice.

The reader will find out that we had to sue the Belgian State to have our US adoption recognized.

When doing research for our court case at the time, I discovered the work of Professor Elizabeth Bartholet. Professor Bartholet is Morris Wasserstein Public Interest Professor at Harvard Law School, and Faculty Director of the Child Advocacy Program (CAP), which she founded in the fall of 2004.

Professor Bartholet's work covers international adoption among many other topics. She studied the actions and policies of governments and agencies in the adoption field, some of which our family had to endure while suing the Belgian government. It is difficult not to label these actions and policies as anti-adoption, anti-child, and – in the case of the author – also as anti-gay. And the problems transcend Belgium.

The Professor explains how international adoption is under siege. The forces mounting the attack claim the child human rights mantle, arguing that such adoption denies heritage rights and often involves abusive practices. Many nations assert rights to hold onto the children born within their borders, while others (very often in the industrialized West) support those demands citing subsidiarity principles (meaning that adoption, and certainly inter-country adoption should be an exception, and only be allowed when there is no other way to care for the child in casu).

However, Professor Bartholet further states, children's most basic human rights are to grow up in the families that will often be found only in international adoption. On top of that, children have the right to *thrive*, not just survive.

These rights should trump any conflicting state sovereignty rights. Policies restricting international adoption, including in-country holding periods, should be rejected. Neither adoption abuses nor concepts of heritage justify limiting international adoption.

I fully endorse Professor Bartholet's view: international adoption appropriately recognizes children as citizens of a global community with basic human rights entitlements.

FOR WHOM IS THIS BOOK THUS WRITTEN?

For everyone who wants adoptions to work: policy makers at the Flemish and Belgian level and globally, employees of adoption services, magistrates, government officials, and adoptive and birth parents and adoptees. If adoption is to become a fully-fledged, positive and inclusive alternative way to make a family, there is still a lot of work to be done.

For people who would like to believe that in our country Belgium, with its progressive legislation, the struggle for equal rights for LGBTs and other minority groups has been won. This is not the case. There is still a lot of work to be done before the rights that the law gives us can be realized in concrete, social situations.

For the LGBT community: all of us — interest groups, activists, and LGBT families with or without children — must continue to work together so that the rights we have acquired, often with great difficulty, become firmly anchored in our society. There is still a lot of work to be done.

For everyone who has a deep desire, an enormous project or a seemingly impossible ambition. Our experience has taught us that belief, perseverance and love can move mountains. Don't give up on your dreams!

More from Professor Bartholet through *www.law.harvard.edu/ faculty/bartholet/pubs.php.*

RECOMMENDED READING FROM PROFESSOR BARTHOLET'S WORK:

Books:
- NOBODY'S CHILDREN: ABUSE AND NEGLECT, FOSTER DRIFT, AND THE ADOPTION ALTERNATIVE *(Beacon Press, 1999)*
- FAMILY BONDS: ADOPTION, INFERTILITY, AND THE NEW WORLD OF CHILD PRODUCTION *(Beacon Press, 1999),* originally published as FAMILY BONDS: ADOPTION & THE POLITICS OF PARENTING *(Houghton Mifflin 1993, paperback ed. 1994)*

Articles and Book Chapters:
- "The International Adoption Cliff: Do Child Human Rights Matter?," Chapter in THE INTERCOUNTRY ADOPTION DEBATE: DIALOGUES ACROSS DISCIPLINES, Ballard, Goodno, Cochran, and Milbrandt, eds. *(Cambridge Scholars Publishing, expected 2014)*
- "The Hague Convention: Pros, Cons, and Potential," Chapter in THE INTERCOUNTRY ADOPTION DEBATE: DIALOGUES ACROSS DISCIPLINES, Ballard, Goodno, Cochran, and Milbrandt, eds. *(Cambridge Scholars Publishing, expected 2014)*
- "Creating a Child-Friendly Child Welfare System: Effective Early Intervention to Prevent Maltreatment and Protect Victimized Children," 60 Buffalo L Rev 1323 *(2012),* also available at SSRN
- Elizabeth Bartholet and David Smolin, "The Debate," chapter in INTERCOUNTRY ADOPTION: POLICIES, PRACTICES, AND OUTCOMES, 233 *(Ashgate Publishing 2012).*
- "Race and Child Welfare: Disproportionality, Disparity, Discrimination: Re-Assessing the Facts, Re-Thinking the Policy Options," July 2011, also available at SSRN

- Bartholet, Wulczyn, Barth, & Lederman, "Race and Child Welfare," Chapin Hall at the University of Chicago *(2011)*, also available at SSRN

- "International Adoption: A Way Forward," 55 New York Law School Rev. 687 *(2010-2011)*

- "Permanency Is Not Enough: Children Need the Nurturing Parents Found in International Adoption," 55 New York Law School Rev. 781 *(2010-2011)*

- "Ratification by the United States of the Convention on the Rights of the Child: Pros and Cons from a Child's Rights Perspective," 633 The ANNALS of Amer. Acad. Political and Social Science 80, Special Issue, The Child as Citizen *(2011)*, also available at SSRN. The final, definitive version is available at *http://ann.sagepub.com/content/633/1/80.full.pdf+html*

- "International Adoption: The Human Rights Position," 1 Global Policy 91 *(2010)*, pre-peer-reviewed version available at *http://papers.ssrn.com/sol3/papers.cfm?abstract_id=1446811*

- "International Adoption: The Human Rights Issues," chapter in BABY MARKETS, Michele Goodwin ed. *(Cambridge Univ. Press 2010)*

- "International Adoption: The Child's Story," 24 Ga. St. U. L. Rev. 333 *(2008)*, also available at SSRN

- "International Adoption: Thoughts on the Human Rights Issues," 13 Buff. Hum. Rts. L. Rev. 151 *(2007)*, also available at SSRN

- "Commentary: Cultural Stereotypes Can and Do Die: It's Time to Move on With Transracial Adoption," 34 J. Am. Acad. Psychiatry Law 315-20 *(2006)*, also available at SSRN

- "International Adoption," chapter in CHILDREN AND YOUTH IN ADOPTION, ORPHANAGES, AND FOSTER CARE, Lori Askeland ed.,

ISBN # 0-313-33183-9. Greenwood Publishing Group Inc.(2005), also available at SSRN

- "Guiding Principles for Picking Parents," 27 Harv. Women's L. J. 323 (2004); also published in a slightly revised form as chapter in GENETIC TIES AND THE FAMILY, Rothstein et al, editors, in 2005, also available at SSRN
- Book Review of Rachel F. Moran's "Interracial Intimacy: The Regulation of Race and Romance," 33 Journal of Interdisciplinary History 320 (2002)
- Reply: "Whose Children? A Response to Professor Guggenheim," 113 Harv. L. Rev.1999 (2000), also available at SSRN
- "Taking Adoption Seriously: Radical Revolution or Modest Revisionism?," 28 Cap. U.L. Rev. 77 (1999), also at SSRN

Acknowledgments

Our story has a happy ending, thanks to the many people who helped and supported us. Many of these people were government officials who did what they could because they knew that what was happening to us was neither right nor just.

In particular, our immeasurable thanks go to the Ambassador of the United States (Ret.), Howard Gutman.

Concerning the endeavor of writing this book, I want to thank Joke for her feedback on the first draft; Jeff for the patient reading, rereading, enhancing of many pages; Nadine Van Meerhaeghe, my editor, who always keeps her calm and who always has great suggestions; Bart Abeloos for his very refined and sophisticated layout ideas; Wannes Vandendriessche for the beautiful pictures; Liz, who managed to turn my Dutch writing into proper English.

At last, a heartfelt 'thank you' to Professor Elizabeth Bartholet for her pioneering academic work. Her work has served as an inspiration as well as moral support for me.

Lieven Vandendriessche
August 2014

Prologue – The Senator from Illinois

4 November 2008

Düsseldorf: the first Tuesday of November.

I had been working in Düsseldorf since I had followed my Belgian boss to the head office of a large German distribution company. I had been his faithful lieutenant for many years, and he had made me an offer I couldn't refuse.

But today I wasn't thinking about work. It was the day of the US presidential elections, and for over eighteen months I had been following all the reports on this race with a passion bordering on the obsessive. No other country organizes elections like the US. I have got to know the country a little, as I'm married to an American who turned up in Brussels as an expat ten years ago. My interest in American politics has been honed by years of discussion with my husband. His superior knowledge of US politics and policies meant that I always came off worst in our debates for the first few years of our relationship, but nowadays he no longer dares to contradict my ever-expanding stream of facts, statements, data, polls and statistics.

I have to admit that I was an admirer of Hillary Clinton's campaign: from the wooden YouTube announcement that she was entering the race ("I'm in it to win it" – *No kidding Hillary!*), through the first months of the campaign without a competitor in sight *(Barack who?)*. From the admiring articles in the New York Times and Newsweek about her successful fundraising, organization and leadership, to the first blunders *(who could be arrogant enough to think that it's not necessary to set up a local election team for the primary elections in Iowa?)*, the first thrashing by Barack Obama in the very same Iowa, followed by tears in New

Hampshire *(didn't you sleep well Hill?)*, through the exhausting months of the primary elections, in which Clinton and Obama wrestled each other in a Titanic struggle, right up to her gracious speech at the Democratic Convention at the end of August ("I am a proud supporter of Barack Obama!" *Wow. Gulp.*).

That morning I was already trembling with excitement. I intended to follow the news all day long from the casting of the very first votes on the East Coast to when the results came out in California.

I took the afternoon off, drove from Düsseldorf to Brussels, where Jeff and I live, went home and turned on CNN in the bedroom. I arranged everything around me so that I wouldn't need to get out of bed again.

I was phoned by American friends who were going to cast their votes, proud of their country and their possible involvement in choosing its first black president. I felt with them and felt connected to that great country where everything is possible. I phoned Jeff, who was working in London, several times. He had already voted for Obama by post a few weeks ago. Jeff's parents would also be voting. Although their memories of African-Americans in Detroit, where they grew up poor, were not very positive, they were also going to vote for Barack Obama – because he's 'smart'.

The first election results, or rather the prognoses, started to come in late in the evening European time. You could see by the faces of the reporters and studio guests that this was going to be a night they would never forget The atmosphere was electric!

At 2 am, just after the election booths had closed on the East Coast, the news came in that the large north-eastern state of Pennsylvania had gone to Obama. This is the state where Jeff was born and raised, a real *blue collar* state. This result sounded the death knell for John McCain's presidential ambitions. He would have needed to win a lot of other states definitively if he was still to become president.

I finally fell into a light and restless sleep with the TV still on. I was woken at 5.00 am by the sound of cheering from my TV.

Barack Obama, the young senator from Illinois who had conducted an unprecedented campaign, had just become the forty-fourth president of the United States! It was an incredibly moving moment. I was so proud of my American family and friends.

I watched the people in Millennium Park in Chicago hugging each other, crying, cheering and dancing. For once, black and white were united and celebrating together. I knew the US well enough to realize that this was a great moment of reconciliation for many people, not least for African-Americans. Their faces were shining as they listened to the first words of their new president, who had just lost his grandmother two days earlier. Standing beside him were his beautiful, intelligent wife and their two young daughters.

I had no idea that on that magical night in Chicago a funny, clever, poor, black woman was pregnant with twin girls. A few months later she was to take the most difficult decision of her life and give us the greatest gift that we would ever receive, all because of her undeniable love of her daughters.

1 | "It is going to be difficult for you"

11 June 2007

Jeff and I were lying on the edge of a swimming pool in Tuscany. We were on holiday in a villa that we had rented with two other couples.

We had made a big decision.

We were going to start an adoption procedure which would hopefully lead to us becoming the fathers of a child, or maybe even children.

By that time, we had been together for nine years, and married for the last three of them. We had both built good careers, and had reached a comfortable level of what money and prosperity could offer us.

That autumn, we had bought a flat in London. A few years ago, I would have killed for a project like this: buying, renovating, decorating, choosing kitchen tiles, bathroom accessories, furniture. Now, I discovered that I was not really enjoying it, and the regular trips to London every few weeks soon became irksome.

When I was working in Düsseldorf I always stayed in a hotel. We didn't really need a third place; two homes are already tiring enough.

Our house in Brussels felt too big. Located in a lively neighborhood, with five bedrooms and a cozy urban garden, it had a wonderful atmosphere, and we had held many parties there. But something was missing.

Jeff and I have always talked a lot about our work and the future. We found ourselves talking more often about children. We had no examples within our immediate circle of friends, but we knew a few people in the US, both gay and straight couples, who were raising children, some of them adopted.

We decided that we would also like to do this if it was possible, as a logical next step in our relationship. We thought that we had everything we needed to give a child, or children, a home. We have a great relationship based on shared values and mutual respect and we both want to leave a legacy that is bigger than us.

We were also aware that Jeff's country, the US, has an enormous underbelly, where children are being born and raised in deprived circumstances, without any support from their biological parents due to a combination of poverty, violence, and a lack of education and opportunities.

All these thoughts were racing through my mind as I prepared to mail our adoption application to the department that organizes courses on international adoption. I looked out over the serene open pastoral Italian landscape and pressed 'send'.

11 September 2007

Today saw the start of our "preparatory course for international adoption", to be held for several days over the course of the next month.

I had been looking forward to it, but Jeff had been more sceptical, saying "There's no course in the world that can prepare us for parenthood." He had a point.

The course dealt with a number of classic adoption issues, such as bonding, openness, how to approach your child's roots, etc.

During these weeks, the realization grew in us that we were ready to become parents. We also realized that we had the right attitude: we didn't expect everything to go perfectly, and we didn't have a long list of criteria that our children had to fulfil.

The 'curriculum' was taught by a friendly woman, buxom and enthusiastic, in a warm and engaging manner.

One day, just before the break, she gave us a hand-written letter with the prophetic words: "My government will not consider it proper for me to do this, but here are the contact details of a few LGBT parents. It is going to be difficult for you to adopt as a couple. I advise you to join forces."

I was surprised by this. Jeff and I had heard stories about discrimination against homosexuals trying to adopt, but I had always taken them with a pinch of salt. Surely if we could show throughout the process that we would be great parents no one would try to stop us. Not when there are so many children in this world in need of a home?

After completing the course, Jeff and I submitted an application form to the Juvenile Court in Brussels, requesting social services to commence the screening process to establish our suitability to adopt. This meant that in the coming months we would be thoroughly assessed by social workers and psychologists. I had read some alarming stories on the internet about this, but decided not to worry.

I was left with another thought after the end of our course: I had noticed that most of our fellow course members had a great attitude to their adoption process. I think I had expected a group full of frantic couples with fertility problems who were desperate to adopt, come hell or high water. But that was not the case at all. I saw real commitment, based on a deep respect for all children in need of a family, no matter where in the world they came from.

For some reason, the course did not pay much attention to

the fact that there are so many children in this world in need of a good home.

One thing was certain. As a gay couple, the countries we could adopt from were limited: the US, South Africa, a few European countries (but these countries – for example, the UK – 'do not make their nationals available for international adoption projects'). Since a recent amendment to Belgian law had made it possible for LGBT couples to adopt, we were all set to be pioneers in international adoption. If we had known then what we know now...

4 August 2008

Today we received a house call as part of the social services investigation into whether we would be suitable adoption parents.

We had already been told that there would be four interviews held over four consecutive weeks.

That, however, is about all we knew. When I phoned the department that would be conducting the investigation in May, I received a rather grumpy answer to an inquiry as to how we could best prepare for the interviews: "Well, you do know the interviews will be about adoption, don't you?" That was as much detail as we were given.

In preparation, we had to submit our life stories. The maximum length was 10 pages, and we managed to fill them without any bother. It did make me wonder how less articulate families would have managed this task.

I hadn't been able to sleep a wink that night (OK, I slept for one and a half hours). At 5.30 am I was in the kitchen baking apple pie. Surely even critical or homophobic social workers and psychologists must like apple pie?

Our house was immaculate, with fresh flowers everywhere. I had displayed extra photos to emphasize the family vibe and leave no doubt as to our "family mindedness".

Jeff and I were well prepared for a host of difficult questions, but I was still racked with nerves. It felt like being back at university just before my finals.

At twenty past nine (ten minutes early!) the doorbell rang.

I opened the door to a middle aged blonde woman. She smiled and I breathed a sigh of relief – maybe she wasn't a homophobic monster after all.

She introduced herself as a social worker and part of the team that would be investigating whether we were suitable to adopt. I took her coat, and we sat down at the table. She said yes to a cup of coffee and told us that she wanted to get to know us a bit better today on the basis of our life stories.

This was the start of a conversation that continued uninterrupted for three and a half hours. It was intense and exhausting, but it went well. There was just one thing which did not go according to plan: when asked about the experience of loss in our lives, my mother's chronic illness came up and I could not hold back my tears. I cursed myself inwardly for showing my weak spot, but Jeff reassured me, saying "After all, they will want to see that we are not cold hearted, won't they"? We are human beings!"

As homework for the next session in a week's time, the social worker asked us to "describe the dynamics of our relationship; the differences and similarities" and to think about "the challenges of sibling adoption".

We finished with a tour of our home (including the possible children's rooms).

It wasn't until later that afternoon that I realized my home baked apple pie was lying untouched in the kitchen.

11 August 2008

The second session with the same social worker was held at the offices of the social services investigation department. She sat in a large armchair. Jeff and I sat opposite her, each in a comfortable chair. We were too far apart to hold hands. Between us and the social worker was a coffee table with coffee, sugar, milk and biscuits. We discussed our homework from the previous session and the possibility of adopting more than one child at a time, as well as our personality differences and the ways in which we complement each other. The conversation was quite relaxed until the social worker said: "Obviously, I know the gay world. This is why I am asking you the following question: do you have extra-marital relationships with other men?" I was so horrified that the words were out of my mouth before my brain could control them: "You mean sexual?" The social worked nodded. "No, no of course not!" Jeff and I answered simultaneously. I stretched out my hand but could not reach him.

Walking back to the car afterwards, Jeff said: "Unbelievable! Do you think they have the nerve to ask straight couples that question?"

18 - 25 August 2008

Our next two appointments were in the same office, but this time with the psychologist, a breezy young woman with a friendly expression. Her questions expanded on the two previous sessions, but the conversations were shorter. She told us that the interviews had gone well so far, and promised that we could expect a copy of the social investigation report before the end of September. The original report would be sent to the juvenile judge. Once it had been received, we would be summoned to a hearing at the Juvenile Court.

Half-way through October we received a copy of the report. I tore open the envelope and went straight to the last page. And there it was: "mature ... couple ... well able to cope with responsibilities ... protective factors ... recommend that they are suitable to adopt one or two children."

We jumped for joy. That was one obstacle out of the way!

14 November 2008

This was the date for our appearance at the Juvenile Court in Brussels. The court was to assess our suitability to adopt, aided by the report from the social services investigation.

I knew who our judge was going to be (a woman) and had asked around about her in my circle of legal friends. She had a reputation for being "strict but fair".

We sat in the waiting room with several other couples who were there for the same reason. They were all interesting people, and it was nice to swap experiences with them.

Then we were called in.

The judge greeted us with a friendly smile. "I have to tell both of you that I have rarely seen such a positive report about prospective adoption parents. Well done!"

I had difficulty concentrating after this compliment; the judge asked a few more innocent questions.

She concluded, saying: "We will deliberate on the case today, but of course you know that my decision will contain good news for you. But it will not be easy for you to adopt because of your specific situation. I wish you all the best. I would like to ask you something else: if your adoption procedure is not successful, would you please consider becoming foster parents? There is an enormous need for people like you."

The judge's last words were to linger in my mind for months. Surely foster care is entirely different to adoption? Why should we then consider it as a back-up plan?

The decision concerning our suitability arrived two weeks later. In long-winded legal jargon, it declared that we were suitable to adopt one or two foreign children.

The process so far had taken us one and a half years. We resolved that we would be the first gay *couple* in Belgium to adopt children from abroad.

6 January 2009
Jeff and I had not been idle since we were declared fit to adopt by the juvenile court.

To start off with, I phoned every official foreign adoption service in Flanders (there are only five). I wanted to know whether it was really true that no one wanted to put gay couples on their waiting list. As it turned out, it was true: the standard answer was that the countries of origin they work with do not acknowledge or want gay adoption. Nor will they work with gay couples on their list; this would be putting them at risk of losing "access" to a country. One of the agencies said something vague about a trial dossier with the US, but that we could not expect to hear anything until the end of the year "because we have enough work already".

We also made dozens of phone calls and sent scores of e-mails to adoption authorities and agencies just about everywhere in the world (at least that's what it felt like).

Many of these were in the US, in states where LGBT couples or singles can adopt.

We'd had a number of telephone conversations with adoption workers and agencies from the State of New York to California. We had also contacted an adoption agency in Chicago, Illinois. Our first contact with this small organization had been warm and cordial. We were given an idea of the work that the agency was doing in the Chicago area, the birth parents that they have experience with, and the situations of the children in need in and around the city. The organization provides assistance to families in difficulties in the general sense. It has several flats in the area of its offices (a gift from a wealthy benefactor) for families in need of temporary accommodation. And yes, every so often there were pregnant women in one of the apartments who did not know which way to turn. The organization tries to work with these people to get their lives back on track. The agency, which has accreditation from both the State of Illinois and the Federal authority for inter-country adoption, is regularly contacted by women who cannot keep their children (this is a bold statement, and we were later to learn that the reality behind it is usually a life with no opportunities, blighted by ill health, a lack of education, heartbreak, poverty and lack of prospects, but nevertheless also blessed with love, hope and wisdom). Jeff and I both felt the positive energy when we were talking to the social workers at the other end of the line. These people were sincere, honest, and compassionate, they knew what they were talking about and they had respect for both the birth parents and the children in need. These were people that we wanted to work with.

In the meantime, almost a year had passed since the US had ratified the Hague Adoption Convention, joining a list of countries (Belgium among them) that had agreed to comply with a number of important rules concerning inter-country adoption. The Convention's primary objective is to safeguard "the best interests of the child", and it stipulates that inter-country adoption must not be the first or only option that is considered for children who are in need (known as the subsidiarity principle). It also imposes a number of rules on the states that have signed the Convention regarding matters where collaboration is mandatory.

One would think this Convention would enable participating countries to establish international adoption processes, which move quickly and are of a high standard. Unfortunately, this is not the case – as we would later learn.

After the Convention had entered into effect [in the United States], the new rules were once more explained clearly on the websites of the American Federal Adoption Authorities and the State Department, in addition to a number of exceptions concerning adoption that applied to Citizens of the United States.

One of the exceptions was that even if American citizens are living abroad, they can adopt a US citizen in the US *as if they are living in the US at the time of adoption.* In this situation, the authorities of the various states in the US, the courts and the federal governments will consider the adoption *as a domestic US adoption.* As far as content goes, the rules for adoption in the US are much the same as those for inter-country adoption *from outside* the US: both are based on the child's interests, adoption can never be considered as the most obvious solution, a court must always be involved and it is strictly illegal to pay for children. For us, this exception clause by the American government meant that we had an alternative to inter-country adoption from Belgium: as an American citizen, Jeff was eligible to adopt internally within the US!

It had become obvious at that point that our plan for an inter-country adoption via Belgian adoption agencies and processes was extremely unlikely to become a reality.

To make sure that we had understood everything properly we made further inquiries about the rule with lawyers in the US and Belgium. No one raised any objections: the guidelines of the federal adoption agencies in Washington DC were crystal clear. They explained to us that the main purpose of this regulation was to give the many US families living abroad the opportunity to adopt in their homeland as if they had always lived there.

We concluded that we would work with the agency in Chicago. We started getting our dossier in order under the US requirements. Intake interviews with a social worker (our "case worker" Corinna*) followed. We had to fill in stacks of documents, and get ready to prove that we were fit to adopt all over again, this time for a court in Illinois.

The formalities included a long questionnaire, in which we had to state our own limits regarding adoption. Would we be prepared to live with a child whose mother had used drugs or alcohol while pregnant? Could we accept a child with a physical handicap or a developmental disability? All these topics were handled without any taboo, in a typically American way. At first I was embarrassed (the Belgian in me found it rather confrontational) but later I understood that the list had forced us to think – once more – about topics that I can't imagine being raised in Belgium without making everyone around the table blush.

In many developing countries there is no point asking such questions, simply because there is often virtually no information provided about the child. This is not the case in the US. I know that some Americans can be put off when they find out too much (for example, the mother was a drug addict or the pregnancy was the result of violence).

Fortunately, Jeff and I are on the same page about this: if we start drawing up a list of our ideal child, where will it end? I am so happy that we always agree about the big things in life, my dear husband and I. And as my sister, who has a daughter, says "Do you think that I drew up a wish list of characteristics I wanted my child to have before I got pregnant?"

But then we received a warning from our case worker: we were not to cherish any false hopes, because not all birth parents will consent to their child being adopted by LGBT parents. Experience shows that some candidates have to wait for months, even years, before they even come up for consideration. For some people that day never comes. "It's just so that you know", she says.

10 *February* 2009

Despite the resistance from the Belgian "system" we perhaps naively continued to explore options through the Belgian administration.

We had an appointment with the adoption officer for the Flemish part of Belgium; a position that was only created two years ago.

About a year or so ago, our lawyer, Mr Deboutte*, had assisted a gay couple who considered that they had not been treated properly by this adoption officer. Their story was in every newspaper in the region. Most of the adoption coverage since that incident had also been negative. In one instance a local foreign adoption service stopped operating after running out of funds, but the adoption officer 'forgot' to tell the candidates registered with it until it was too late.

In the case of the gay couple represented by our lawyer, the adoption officer's department had withheld the file from the American adoption service for months (even though there is a legal maximum term) before rejecting it, offering practically no justification for its decision. Even after external pressure forced them to re-examine the case, they still refused to grant approval. The couple never found out why.

So there we were, with this infamous adoption officer in the head office of the Government Agency Kind en Gezin (Child and Family) in Brussels, curious to find out the current stance regarding adoption in the US. Jeff was very combative, and I wasn't planning on sitting around passively either. I just don't get it: Belgium has no problem with adoption from countries that have *not* signed the Hague Convention [which contains the most protections for children in need], but apparently cannot consider adoptions from the US?

Our lawyer attended the meeting with us, but not to do the talking: we wanted to do that ourselves.

The adoption officer entered with a young woman at her side, apparently Child and Family's adoption lawyer.

The meeting was a disaster. We had a list of pertinent questions. What are the standards or guarantees expected from a potential adoption contact in the US? What problems have been identified which must be assessed in advance? What are the objections that have led to you being unable to approve proposals for US adoption channels in the past? What contacts do you have in the US? How will the Flemish adoption officer ensure that LGBTs are not discriminated against by being excluded from foreign adoption policy? But in the two hours the meeting lasted, these questions were pretty much ignored. My emotions shifted from hopeful optimism through irritation to being scarcely able to contain my indignation: this woman did not take us seriously and it was definitely her intention to send us away empty handed. She had no intention of finding out, either now or in the future, if it would be possible to work with the US. She was smart enough not to suggest at any point that she had anything against same sex couples wanting to adopt, but I could feel it in my bones that she did not like homosexuals. I'm not a touchy feely type, but I just *knew* that this woman did not really approve of adoption in general. But in that case, what on earth was she doing in charge of Belgian adoption policy? I was appalled.

Her answers were consistently vague: she "had heard stories" about a lot of money changing hands in the US for the adoption of certain children. (When asked where she had heard this, her only reply was "We have our sources".) She "suspected" that there was not enough attention in the US to the subsidiarity principle (meaning it is too easy to adopt children who could have otherwise grown up perfectly happily in their original family). She "had heard" that there were lawyers in the US operating at the edge of the law. (How? And who?) She had no useful information whatsoever about her study trip to the US over a year ago, but could only say "we made contacts". She could not recommend anyone who might work with us ("but if we find a reliable adoption channel we will be sure to let you know"; *yeah right).* For the rest, she mainly used terms like "problems", "exceptions" etc.

When the Child and Family lawyer – a rather sharp young woman – began to lecture us in a pedantic manner on the content of the Hague Convention (Hello! Jeff and I both have a legal background) Jeff – who is usually calm personified – had had enough. This woman was practically accusing the US of child trafficking and paying for babies! Our lawyer (good job he came after all) and I were able to calm him down, but one thing was clear: no good was going to come of this meeting. We were seen as troublemakers, and these people could not get us out of there quickly enough.

If anyone thought it would ever be possible for a gay couple in Flanders to adopt a child from abroad while this woman was in charge of policy, they had another thing coming. Time was to prove me right.

Jeff was furious: "How is it possible that this woman is the face of adoption in this country?" There was nothing I could say in reply. It had been the most disheartening meeting I had ever had in my life – at least, up to that point.

We were to hear more of this person: a few years later she was nominated for Çavaria's (the gay rights group) homophobia award. During a hearing of the Flemish Parliament about the new adoption decree, she uttered the following words of wisdom: "Oh, it's just my personal opinion, but if all those parents who are so eager to adopt children from abroad gave their money to local development projects, they could help 30 children instead of just adopting one."

Well that's a classic coming from an adoption official! However, all that was still in the future at this point. One thing was clear, however: our only hope of making a family lay in the US, a country that was, in theory, much less progressive than self-assured Belgium, with its supposedly progressive social and legal treatment of the gay community.

2 | "Congratulations, dad!"

Jeff's parents were in Brussels, staying with us for a week.

Today we had planned a trip to Delft. Americans are familiar with the blue and white ceramics and Delft is a charming city with just enough to do and see there to make it a good destination for a day trip. Another important reason for going to Delft was that it is in the Netherlands, so going there would allow *Mom and Dad* to cross another country off their "Been There" list.

That afternoon we were sitting at a pavement cafe in the market square, enjoying the sunshine, when Jeff's telephone went. It was probably work, nothing unusual. Jeff excused himself and went to take his call somewhere quieter while we ordered.

It was more than ten minutes before Jeff returned. His face was white, and all he could say was: "O my God. It was Chicago. I have to go to the toilet." He went indoors and we were left sitting there, stunned.

When he finally returned he was still dazed. The phone call hadn't been about work; it was our *case worker,* Corinna, on the line to tell us that we might be about to become the fathers of twins. Twin girls.

There was a woman in a clinic in Chicago who was thirty-two weeks pregnant. She had to stay in bed to prevent her twins being born prematurely. She had told the hospital's social workers that she was considering giving her daughters up for adoption. The hospital's social workers had contacted the adoption agency, and the adoption agency contacted us.

Jeff was not his usual calm self. Corinna had urged him to remember that nothing was definite. There was a whole list of practical and legal conditions we had to fulfil before we could actually adopt.

I immediately felt a deep compassion for this unknown woman in Chicago. She was the mother of the girls who might become our daughters, but I didn't even know her name. I tried to imagine how it must feel for her, all alone in a hospital; waiting, trying to rest for the sake of her unborn daughters, and on top of all that trying to decide what was the best future for them – even if that meant a heart-breaking separation. I hoped that she had someone to confide in. Hopefully she did not have to go through this all on her own.

Corinna had limited information so she agreed to call back later that evening once she had found out more.

Mom and Dad were beaming. "Such great news! Two grandchildren!" I sat there in a kind of trance, wanting to get home straight away. But Mom still wanted to buy souvenirs – for the entire family as it turned out – so we stayed in Delft for a few more hours. I was functioning more or less on automatic pilot.

It was quiet on the journey home. A thousand thoughts flashed through my mind, among them: it's too soon to be happy yet.

Once home, we sat down at the dining table. Jeff's parents had considerately retired to their room. We picked up the phone. "Hey guys!" said Corinna's cheerful voice. She repeated more or less what we already knew, and impressed on us that although there was a chance ('fifty-fifty') it was still too early to book our plane tickets. She gave us information about the birth mother's social and medical history, as this would explain the context of the adoption and help us to understand the reasons for it if it went ahead. Her story made me realize how fortunate I had been all my life, with the opportunities and health I had been given. I nudged Jeff to ask what color the birth mother was: African-American. My heart gave a little leap of excitement.

I blurted out that I could not imagine ever giving up my children for adoption. Corinna was silent, then she said: "Lieven, I have been doing this job for eleven years. I have two sons and I can't imagine it either. But then, I haven't had the life that many of the birth mothers I meet have had. That life is the context within which they make the best decisions they can for their children." I will never forget those wise words.

Corinna did not have any contact with 'our' birth mother. In our agency, the roles are divided between the social workers who act as contact persons for adoptive parents and those who look after the birth parents. This distance is a precautionary measure. The birth parent's social workers need to be able to search for the best solution for the child, together with the birth parent, without having to consider the wishes of prospective adoptive parents. In this case, that was us.

Jeff and I needed time to recover after that telephone call.

The birth was to be delayed for as long as possible, but the doctors didn't think that the babies would wait for another month and a half. They would probably arrive in just one or two weeks.

I phoned my sisters, brother and parents, and asked them to keep the news to themselves for just a while longer. My sister was excited; maybe there were going to be two new nieces in the family! My brother is always a man of few words, but I could hear the emotion in his voice. Talking to my father, I could hear that he still did not dare to believe the good news.

Düsseldorf, Monday morning. D-Day. I was so nervous that I could hardly keep my mind on my work.

We had found out a few days earlier that the birth was to be induced today. It felt so strange that we could not let ourselves be totally happy: Corinna kept reminding us that there was still a real possibility that the adoption would not proceed. The law in Illinois stipulates that a woman may not relinquish her parental rights until three days after the birth. Corinna had told us that it would not be wise to buy baby things or decorate a nursery. I struggled to keep my emotions under control.

This past weekend, we spent in London, fretting nervously about what would happen; including panic attacks from both of us. Together with our good friends Mark and Nigel, we also went to see "Priscilla, Queen Of The Desert"- The Musical. The contrast between the play on stage and our internal turmoil could not have been greater!

I surfed to websites about Chicago, the South Side, African-American hair care for girls, et cetera. I read a lot, but remembered practically nothing. I felt as though I mustn't.

A few of my colleagues in Düsseldorf knew what was going on. I had already informed my boss that I might be going to the US at the end of the week for an indefinite period. He is the devoted father of three children and wished me all the best.

Because of the time difference (seven hours) it might be late before we heard anything.

Somehow I got through the day, and that evening I had dinner with a good friend and colleague.

Back at my hotel room I switched on the television. It was 10 pm when the phone rang. It was Jeff in London. "They've been born!" I could hear the tears in Jeff's voice. "Corinna phoned. They both seem healthy! One is bigger than the other!" I tried to write down as much information as possible. We converted the weight into kilos: Twin A (info from the hospital) weighed 1.36 kilo. Her larger sister, Twin B, weighed 1.81 kg. Twin A had an Apgar score of 8-9, and her sister had 7-8.

I called our family doctor. I have her mobile number and am allowed to contact her at any time. She answered immediately, bless her, and listened to my incoherent story before saying that it sounded as if both babies were strong. She explained that Apgar scores give a quick impression of a new-born baby's general condition (breathing, muscle tone etc.).

I got back to Jeff with this reassuring information.

We felt a huge mix of emotions, but the main one was relief. And maybe just a spark of hope.

After a restless night, the morning brought few answers..

28 June 2009
Sunday, and the day I was about to leave for Chicago.

Last Thursday, three days ago and as soon as it was legally possible, the birth mother transferred custody of her children to our adoption agency in Chicago and definitively relinquished her parental rights.

We booked our tickets immediately. I wanted to be on the next available flight, which was today. Jeff planned to join me in Chicago two days later. He had arranged to take six months off work, but first he had to tie up a few loose ends at the office. I had taken a month's holiday for the time being, and for the rest we reckoned that we would take things as they came. At any rate, we made sure that our return tickets were flexible.

On Saturday evening Jeff and I went out to dinner with just the two of us for the last time before becoming parents, to an Italian in our neighborhood. I could not eat a bite, and just drank wine. I watched the people around me laughing, eating and drinking, enjoying the lovely summer evening.

It was not the first time that I had flown to the States on my own, but this time I felt really lonely. I hid my feelings, as it was bad enough for Jeff that he could not come with me, and he was being so sweet and attentive (You are sure you have your passport... the address in Chicago... the phone number of the adoption agency etc.).

My aunt Magda had given us a first gift for the girls; two cuddly toys – one orange and one pink. What a sweet and considerate thing to do.

I generally like to drink a few glasses of wine when I travel long distance; it helps me to nod off or relax. I didn't dare to this time as I didn't want to be getting off the plane with alcohol on my breath. (After all, I still had to meet the director of the adoption agency. He was going to give me the keys to an apartment we could rent during our visit. This was the agency's idea, as a hotel would be expensive and less cozy). Just imagine if after meeting us they decided we were unsuitable types!

I couldn't relax. I kept thinking of the girls – my daughters. What if they turned out to be so ugly I would be unable to love them... I had dared to confess this thought to my sister, who roared with laughter. "But Lieven, don't you realize that every mother has this thought? But then your child is born and it's love at first sight." But the firmness with which she asserted this didn't completely calm my fears.

We didn't have to spend long thinking up names for our children. Once we knew that our daughters-to-be (we hoped) would be African-American, we drew up a shortlist of three names with links to the black American community: Ella, Maya and Nina.

Ella for Ella Fitzgerald. Jeff and I love her glorious voice with its lust for life. Fitzgerald had a long career and is respected all over the world. We had also discovered another Ella, Ella Jenkins, the singer-songwriter from Chicago who is well known there for her beautiful children's music drawn from her African-American roots.

Maya for the writer, activist and black role model Maya Angelou. I have been an admirer of her work for a long time, and I particularly love her poetry. Years ago, I was deeply moved by her beautiful autobiographical novel "I Know Why The Caged Bird Sings". Angelou is a wise woman who has made no secret in the many interviews she has given of her support for the LGBT struggle for equal rights in the US.

Nina for Nina Simone. But then Jeff discovered that she had had serious problems with the American Tax Authorities. Jeff has had a career dealing with Corporate Tax issues for 20 years, and he didn't want to name one of his daughters after someone who had been accused of tax evasion (his words, not mine).

Ella and Maya sound good in both Dutch and English and – let's not forget – French. Since we live in Brussels, this is also important.

On the plane, I poured my heart out to a sympathetic stewardess. She congratulated me and treated me with the smooth reassurance that I expect from an American professional, which was just what I needed to believe on this occasion: everything was going to be just fine.

As it turned out she must have been clairvoyant. One month later she was once again to be our stewardess on the flight from Chicago to Brussels, our first transatlantic flight with our daughters.

I arrived at O'Hare Airport. Not all of my Border Control moments with the American Immigration Authorities since 9/11 have gone smoothly. The border guards at US airports sometimes do their work so thoroughly in their search for terrorists that they really get on my nerves. Jet lag does not help either of course, and I can't always handle their overzealous inquiries about the reasons for my visit. This time, however, everything ran smoothly; I was soon through Immigration and Customs and into the beautiful, modern and – importantly for someone who can be a dizzy idiot in places like these – easy to find your way around airport.

On arrival, I phoned Ronald*, the director of the adoption agency. I didn't know a thing about Ronald (all contact had been with social workers) but he sounded like the very personification of American cordiality. He told me to go to his house and wait in the garden; he was at a barbecue with friends, but he was on his way.

The taxi brought me to a suburb of Chicago. The houses were pleasant, but not very big, and some looked better cared for than others. Ronald's house looked chaotic but cozy. There were a few bicycles lying around and the garden chairs in the middle of the lawn looked very inviting. The garden was lush, and not too obsessively tended. Very Bohemian, I thought to myself. I sat down on a comfortable chair with my luggage beside me (well, Ronald had said I could).

Ronald soon arrived with his wife in a vintage convertible. He looked exactly as he had sounded: a warm, lively man in his late fifties. He had round glasses, gray curls, and sandals (when we got to know him better we found out that he had a hippie past which had even included a youthful adventure in Amsterdam). His wife was a pretty brunette who seemed to be accustomed to her husband taking center stage when they had company.

Once the formal courtesies were out of the way (yes, I'd had a good flight; no delays, no storms on the way, no I was not too tired), followed by the ritual of present giving (Belgian chocolates of course) Ronald invited me to take a drive with him through the neighborhood. He said he would drop me off at our apartment, which was above the adoption agency.

It was a lovely sunny summer day in Chicago. The skyline stood out in contrast against the bright blue sky. We drove along Lake Shore Drive in the convertible, from the north to the center of the city. Although my thoughts kept wandering off to the two little girls waiting for us, I enjoyed the wind in my hair and the sun on my face. The city had a relaxed, friendly atmosphere and, thanks to its generous layout, it didn't feel too busy. The beach at Lake Michigan gives Chicago a holiday atmosphere all summer long. Its citizens can enjoy the lovely weather every day, knowing that it will not be the only day they'll be able to spend on a sunny beach. I was to learn that this is something of a metaphor for the natural disposition of the Chicagoans.

Ronald dropped me off at the apartment; a spacious, second floor flat. The living room looked out onto the street. Behind it was a hallway, off which were two bedrooms and a bathroom. At the back, there was a large kitchen with a dining area. It was not exactly luxurious (after all, this is a non-profit organization), and the walls could have done with a lick of paint here and there. But

I was too tired and grateful to fuss about details like that.

Ronald said he would collect me the next morning and take me to visit the girls.

When Ronald had left, I called Jeff to tell him all about it. Jeff could hardly wait to leave.

After that I walked around the neighborhood for a while. The building was on a pleasant, quiet street with houses (all with the obligatory front stoops and American flags hoisted against white or pale gray walls) which led onto a large road lined with shops, cafes, restaurants and supermarkets. Although it was a real American urban neighborhood, it was what I would call a somewhat 'alternative' neighborhood (it reminded me of Ronald), which instead of being dominated by chain stores, had feminist bookshops ('Women and Children First') and gay hamburger bars ('Hamburger Mary's'). I was exhausted, so I treated myself to an Apple Martini, congratulating myself on my self-restraint during my journey and the excellent impression that I had undoubtedly made on the director of our adoption agency...

At 7 pm local time, I fell into a deep and dreamless sleep.

29 June 2009

I woke up around 6 am Chicago time. I had a shower, and as there was nothing in the apartment except coffee, I went outside. It was a fresh summer morning; the sun was already up, but the neighborhood was still not fully awake. I noticed again how relaxed the atmosphere in this neighborhood was. I found a café, drank a coffee, took a New York Times and realized to my amazement that I was able to concentrate long enough to read it. For the first time since my arrival I was enjoying myself. I smiled: the days of reading newspapers for hours on end might almost be over. I made a few more calls to the home front and then returned to our adoption agency.

Ronald was going to take me to the hospital where our daughters had been born, at 34 weeks, and where they had to stay until they had gained some weight. I was about to learn a lot about hospitals, medical care and hospital insurance in the US (I had already arranged hospital insurance for the girls during our stay in Chicago through my employer in Germany).

On the way, Ronald explained to me that the girls were in Cook County, a public hospital. This didn't mean a lot to me, and it was not until later that I realized that many people used that hospital either because they could not afford health insurance or were so poor that they were covered by the Medicaid Program (the health insurance scheme for poor people in the US). The hospital is community-focused, which means that it primarily aims to serve people from the immediate surroundings. These are mainly poor people from the notorious South Side of Chicago, infamous in the 1930s for prohibition and the Mafia – but also for jazz music! Ronald told me that the world famous series "ER" was based on this hospital's emergency room, which treats 100,000 patients every year.

My first visit there was a culture shock. Homeless people were sitting around near the entrance, drinking and begging. On the way in I saw a little girl of about three years of age walking in high heels beside her mother. The reception area smelt of sweat, urine and exotic spices (couldn't anyone open a window?) and was hectic and noisy. We first had to register for a day pass at reception, then go through a metal detector before we could get to the lift. We had to go to the Neonatal Intensive Care Unit.

This was where the girls were, and before we could see them, we first had an appointment with the head of social services. It was she who had contacted our adoption agency at the birth mother's request. Dorothy* was an older African-American lady with a gentle demeanor and a soft voice. She had clearly had little experience with white boys from Belgium. Ronald explained that my partner Jeff and I (I wondered how she would react) would like an access pass for as long as our daughters were still in the hospital. I could see by the look on her face that she was finding me every bit as exotic as I was finding her, but she remained friendly and told me not to worry. "I'll make sure you and your ... babydaddy ... can both come here as much as you want." I could hardly suppress a smile.

(Much later, Ronald told me that he had come with me because he had never worked with this hospital before and had no idea how the staff would react to the prospect of two white fathers for two black babies).

Dorothy left us in the capable hands of Annie*, a young social worker who was to take us to see the girls. Although I tried to stay alert, by now I was barely aware of what was going on around me. We arrived at the Neonatal Intensive Care Unit. The first thing I noticed was how neat and new everything was. After the scenes in the entrance hall I had been expecting something else. We had to scrub our hands and arms and put on green coats before we were allowed to enter the rooms where the premature babies lay. Annie led us into a room with twenty small beds, all separate from each other, each with all kinds of machines and wires attached to them. It turned out that there was one nurse for every two beds. The nurses worked in ten-hour shifts, caring for just one or two babies. They monitored whether their babies were eating well, checked their bowel movements, weighed them, etc.

"There." Annie pointed to a nurse standing beside us, holding a tiny baby in both hands. The baby was being held more or less upright and had just eaten. I scanned the information sheet attached to the bed. It said "Twin A". Beside that, handwritten, was the name that the birth mother had given our daughter. I gasped for breath, and then all my attention was drawn to the little girl. It was her.

"Oh, she's lovely" was the first thought to go through my mind. A weight fell from my shoulders! This girl was exquisite! She had a cute little head with a shock of black hair and she looked so peaceful. So beautiful. The nurse told me that she had just had a large feed. I squatted down to get a better look at her face. Such peace, the balance, that wisdom... this was definitely Maya. I had to tell Jeff! The tears rolled down my cheeks and I couldn't stop them. "Congratulations, Dad", said Ronald, who was also moved. At last I was a father.

I was allowed to hold Maya.

Then we asked to see Twin B. She was on the other side of the hallway. This was a shock for me, because that was where the incubators were. The first baby on the left as we entered the room was a lively little girl, who seemed no bigger than my outstretched hand, with a beautifully shaped head and an enchanting little face with full lips that formed a fascinating, beautiful mouth. There was also an information sheet at the end of her bed with a handwritten first name. This little girl was not calm: she was waving her arms and legs to free herself from her blanket. Wow, I thought, she expresses her feelings. She knows what she wants and she'll let you know too! It's Ella, no doubt about it. Our names fitted perfectly, almost as if this was meant to be.

The nurse took Ella out of her incubator. She was so tiny I was scared she might break.

The nurse was called Siwini* and was of Thai origin. "Don't worry, you're a natural" she said as she showed me the best way to hold this tiny being. A while later, I learned how to feed a premature baby weighing less than one and a half kilos with a bottle containing 35 millilitres of milk.

I stayed on. Ronald and Annie had already left.

I was loving it. I didn't bother trying to conceal my emotions. Siwini helped to reassure me. She was clearly bursting with curiosity but she was too polite to ask questions, and I didn't feel the need to discuss my feeling with anyone but those two tiny girls.

The afternoon flew by. I went from one bed to the other, holding each girl in turn. At 6 pm, overcome with exhaustion, I said goodbye to them.

It was not until then that I realized that I had been in the hospital for five hours, during which time I had had no reception on my mobile phone. I needed to call Jeff at once. "Finally! Where were you? Tell me everything!" My poor partner was trying not to sound angry. I could not say much except "They are so beautiful! And I held them!" "For all that time?" "Yes!" Jeff tried to get all sorts of important details out of me but I couldn't say much. "You'll see for yourself tomorrow!"

I slept peacefully that night. Tomorrow Jeff would be here.

30 June 2009

I took a taxi to the hospital early. I just wanted to get to our girls. They were a week old already and I wanted them to feel safe and secure with me.

As I signed the visitor's register in the children's department, I noticed that the girls' birth mother had also been there. I saw her signature on the day after the birth, and then once more on the day that she had signed the document transferring custody to the adoption agency. (I later learned that this was the same day she had left hospital. She had taken a bus back home all alone.) I felt a wave of emotion pass through me. Later on, when our daughters needed to know more about where they came from, we must make sure they understood. They had not been abandoned by their mother. She had not run away from the painful confrontation with her two new-born daughters. She came back to say goodbye. I felt respect, love and a tiny bit of the pain of this amazing woman.

I spent the day with each girl in turn. None of the friendly staff could tell me why they weren't in the same room. I decided to discuss this later with Jeff. We ought to ask if the twins could be allowed to lie beside each other. After all, they'd spent thirty-four weeks together in their mother's womb.

One of the nurses asked: "Are you going to adopt both?" Of course!

There was an exquisitely beautiful blonde baby who was also in an incubator. He just cried and cried. He would still be there when our girls were allowed to leave the hospital several weeks later. Someone told me later that he had been left there by his mother. We discovered that Cody* had a heroin problem due to his mother's addiction during her pregnancy. I will never forget the sight of those eternally patient nurses walking up and down all day with the crying child, trying to comfort him. "This happens a lot here", said Siwini.

Jeff arrived from London that evening. It was already 9.30 by the time he arrived at our apartment in his rented car, but there was no stopping either him, or me, so we drove to the hospital. For once, it was me showing Jeff around the US. Jeff met Ella and Maya and immediately agreed with my choice of names. The nurses met us for the first time as a couple. Not one, but two white guys for the black twins. I could see by the faces of some of the nurses that they had their doubts, but no one said anything.

A week later, one of them came up to me and said "Tell your friends in Europe what you have done. There are so many children born in this hospital who could use a good home."

Later that evening Jeff showed me the notes that he had made on the plane. "What do you think of giving the girls the name of our mothers as second names and the name they received from their birth mother as their third name?" I thought it was a great idea. It was a way to express our feeling that our daughters belonged in our family, and it also meant we could celebrate their roots.

3 | Angelina Jolie

15 July 2009

Our girls had gained enough weight! Today they were leaving the hospital.

In the car, I kept going over the events of the last two and a half weeks in my mind.

We had visited our daughters every day, from after lunch until eight or nine in the evening. Jeff and I swapped every two hours, so that our daughters would get to know both of us. (We would keep this up until they were two: every day that we cared for them together, we would take turns, saying "Today is my Ella/ Maya day!"). We spent our mornings shopping in Chicago, buying tiny baby clothes, phoning friends and family in Europe, trying to deal with work-related e-mails.

Maya's sucking reflex was not yet fully developed – she ate too slowly at first – so she was receiving extra food through a tube in her nose. Her weight increased by 5 grams: I thought this was worrying but the nurse didn't see it as a problem. It was clear that our girls were strong.

The visitors who came to see the babies thought so too. Jeff's mother, who already had seven grandchildren, was indefatigable. Together with Jeff's sister and her boyfriend, she had driven from South Carolina – all through Friday night – to arrive in Chicago on Saturday. Mom was delirious with happiness, and Jeff's sister and brother-in-law took thousands of photos of our two little stars. Mom stayed with us for ten days to give practical help (she said). I shall never forget one episode during her visit; the night we went to Mary's gay hamburger bar.

On that evening, we were driving past Mary's on the way home from the clinic and decided to stop for a bite to eat. Mom clearly thought that sitting in a gay bar with her son and son-in-law was a very rock-and-roll thing to do. As fate would have it, it was bingo night. "My favorite game!" she cheered, so we decided to play a few rounds. 'Mary', an overweight drag queen in towering stilettos, was acting as Master of Ceremonies for this thrilling event. Mary didn't shrink from the use of foul language when it came to issuing instructions and handing out Bingo challenges. I thought it was great fun and Mom was having a whale of a time (partly thanks to two Cosmopolitans). Jeff, however, grew paler and paler with each new challenge that Mary gave us, terrified that his mother would hear too many obscenities for her own good. No need to worry – Mom was too busy flirting with "Bear", a leather-clad guy who looked like he had stepped straight out of the pre-aids era in San Francisco. He thought that our Mom was 'very, very cool'.

Dane, a friend from Washington DC, came to stay for a weekend. Dane loves children even though he does not have any himself, and came bearing gifts and take-away dinners. We also had a visit from another friend who lives in Chicago. Sarah has four children, has always had a career and always looks smiley, happy and relaxed. We think she is the queen of multitasking. Coincidentally, her ex-husband and father of her children is African-American, and when people see her with her mixed-race children, they often congratulate her on her 'beautiful adopted family'. Not only are her teenage children beautiful; they are also smart and quick-witted. We decided they would be great role models for Ella and Maya. I want our children to grow up like that.

As the days passed, the staff gradually began to relate to us differently, their professional, business-like manner abandoned in favor of a more personal, warm and friendly approach. We laughed together, listened to each other, and Jeff and I received a host of tips on how to care for the girls. We were even allowed to spend a night in the hospital with our daughters; the four of us in a separate room. The nurses checked in on us ever two hours to see how we were doing (very well indeed). Downstairs in the foyer, the receptionists asked us how the girls were doing every day.

At first, one nurse with Indian roots could not get over the fact that Jeff and I wanted to learn how to change diapers and dress the girls ourselves. She kept offering to do it for us, and when, finally, she could no longer resist our demands to be shown what to do, she was so patronizing that it was obvious she did not have much faith in us – at least before she got to know us better. But as we were leaving, she told us that she had every confidence that we would be good fathers. She had already confided in us that in her family, fathers do not care for their babies, as that is seen as the task of mothers and grandmothers.

Dr. Fong*, the paediatrician in charge of the NICU, had unleashed a barrage of questions during the first few days. "What are you going to call the babies? Are you going to give up work now? Are you married?" At first I thought this was a bit over-the-top, but I gradually came to understand that the doctor had never seen a family like ours before. Her questions did not arise out of contempt or distrust, but concern. She was a lovely woman. She had tears in her eyes as we left, and congratulated us on our dedication.

I also remember the nurse who had to teach all the new parents cardio-pulmonary resuscitation in case their children choked on their food, or something (I never understood that; don't children in Europe have accidents like this?) Jeff and I had to practice on dolls. The nurse did her best, but could not suppress a smile as she finally placed a tick in our file. We promised her faithfully that we would repeat the course once we were back in Belgium.

Yesterday evening, as we left 'our' unit in the hospital, we were stopped by a heavily built African-American nurse who asked us in a menacing tone: "Are you the guys adopting the twins?" "Yes", our voices quivered. She beckoned to us. Then enveloping both of us in her enormous arms and pressing us against her, while the tears rolled down her and our cheeks, she said: "Thank you for what you are doing. You know, Angelina Jolie runs around the world adopting children from everywhere, while so many children in the US need a good home. Thank you for doing this." Afterwards we thought that we must have been quite a sight: two sissies in a big hug by a nurse!

During our time at the hospital I noticed how few visits there were to some of the little beds in the ward. One incubator held a tiny boy who was even smaller than our Ella. One day a young girl, who didn't even look sixteen, tottered into the ward in impossibly high heels. Despite the nurse's protests (the baby had just eaten and gone to sleep) she picked the little guy out of the incubator, changed him into an outfit that she had fished out of her shopping bag and put him back in. She immediately grabbed her things and left again, accompanied by her boyfriend who also looked like a child. The nurse sighed and tried to comfort the little boy, who was now crying, back to sleep.

When we had to go past the children's unit security officer, this time with our baby car seats as we were finally picking up the girls, she asked "Are you going home with the girls?" We answered yes. She said "God bless you and your girls. Good for you. I have no problem with that. I don't hate."

We arrived at the ward. I had a cake with me (for thirty people – only in America). It was for the staff, to thank them for their excellent care and the warmth which with they had treated us. We had so much to thank these women for and I will never forget them.

Siwini was still our biggest fan: before we left she took photos of the four of us. Jeff and I held the babies against our skin ("kangaroo-care"). It was for an information poster to be displayed on the ward to inspire other families with premature babies. Great eh? She also gave us photos that she had taken during our daughters' stay (Siwini always carries a small printer around at work, as she earns a little extra income by photographing families with their babies. "Normally I charge two dollars per picture, but for you guys it's free.").

The goodbyes were emotional; it was like something out of an American film, with lots of "We love you", "Bless you", "Good luck", but without being sentimental or cloying. We left our e-mail address and promised to stay in touch and send photos regularly. And then we fastened Ella and Maya into their seats for their very first car journey.

20 July 2009
I woke up early because I was too nervous to sleep. Today we were due to appear with our daughters before the Family Court in Chicago.

Ella and Maya were doing so well. They were getting big, and were feeding eight times a day (which meant not much sleep for us). I was keeping minute records of how much they drank and when they had a bowel movement (a week or so later in Belgium, when I informed my family doctor of my administrative zeal, she just looked at me, rolled her eyes and said "Just cut that out immediately, would you?").

Over the past few days we had slipped easily into a routine: everything revolved around feeding and we just slept whenever we could. The first bath time – trauma for Ella, Maya, Papa and Daddy, roars of laughter for Grammy. Our first walk outside was also memorable. Ella and Maya each fitted easily into a kind of pouch that we carried on our sides. Jeff was terrified that they would suffocate, and could not relax for a minute. I was totally relaxed about drinking a glass of wine 'wearing' our little bundles in a wine bar. We were stopped in the street by a curious woman: "Are those your puppies?" Well, madam, that's one way of putting it, I suppose.

The best thing was that if felt as if the four of us were made to be together. I felt so complete. Our girls just fitted into our family like pieces into a jigsaw puzzle. Jeff was also excelling himself as a father, and the bond between us was stronger than ever.

Was this too good to be true?

We got ready to go to court. Our lawyer had explained to us what was going to happen. We were to appear before the judge to apply for guardianship (which had been held up to that point by the adoption agency). In all likelihood the court would consent to this. This would then initiate six-month probationary period, after which, if all went well, the adoption would become final under American law. In the intervening period, the judge would have to receive four reports, written by an American social worker who evaluates American families in Europe both before and after adoption procedures (so this social worker was to visit us in Brussels). Even if everything went well today it was still too soon to relax. The procedure in Illinois is extremely strict, to prevent adoptions becoming too casual a process. Remember these words.

Our attorney, Maureen*, did everything possible to reassure us, without glossing over the obstacles. She is an adoption specialist in Chicago, and president of a national organization of family lawyers, who specializes in adoption law. We felt good with her because she was obviously not doing this job for money, but out of a great sense of social commitment. She gives free lectures in Illinois and further afield about adoption and adoption-related subjects.

In the waiting room at the courthouse it looked like adoption day. We met three other adoptive families. Once more, I found that adoption is considered perfectly normal in the US, both by the law and socially. In Belgium I often have the feeling that a stigma still clings to adoption, not so much in public opinion, but administratively and politically. But here adoption seemed something to be proud of! It is a fully-fledged alternative way of creating a family, in the eyes of both the government and society. We also noticed this with the judge; a tall woman, aged around fifty. She looked at our girls (they were sleeping, as good as gold) and asked a few questions. When she heard that we live in Brussels, she said "Oh, I've been through Belgium on holiday" She mentioned Bruges, Ghent and Brussels. She wished us all the best and congratulated all four of us on our family. Jeff was now Ella and Maya's legal guardian.

As far as the American authorities were concerned, today's

procedure was a purely domestic affair.

On the way from the courthouse to the car park we were stopped by passers-by who could see the look of pride on our faces. "Congratulations guys!" "You guys are so lucky! Cute girls!" In the car park, the attendant, an older African-American man, came up to us and asked if we had adopted the girls. When we said yes, he replied: "Thanks for doing that guys. You are going to give them a great life." Well, actually, we knew it was us who were the lucky ones, but I thought it was very kind of him.

I was struck by the positive reactions of many African-Americans to our family. I couldn't help thinking that the election of their president had had a healing effect on the way they were able to look at the world. Adopting our daughters had also made us a 'family of color'. I thought it was fantastic.

29 July 2009
Arrival at Zaventem with our daughters.

The past week in Chicago had been hectic. On top of caring for the girls, which was already intensive (no one apart from us was allowed to touch our girls) we had to prepare for our journey to Belgium.

Extra suitcases were purchased, passports were ordered, little clothes and baby items were gathered together along with a thousand other things that you don't have to think about when you only have yourself to look after. I loved the logistical challenge that our new family presented. My professional, rational mind saw it as a project for which all the deliverables were perfectly foreseeable and measurable. The girls were given milk every three hours, and as I couldn't sterilize bottles on the plane, I had a supply that would not have looked out of place in a World War III type contingency plan. "If you fail to prepare, you prepare to fail".

At Chicago airport we experienced the magic that our children could work. After checking in our baggage, (the stewardess kindly turned a blind eye to our excess weight), the security agents waved us past a horribly long queue. We were put through the security process quickly. Female agents cooed over our daughters, and the men congratulated us. And what made me proudest of all: one of the guys (moustache, stern face) picked us out of the queue, saying "You guys are a family with infants? Come on through here!" It gave me a wonderful, complete feeling to see that the rest of the world understood that we were inextricably linked to these two tiny, helpless bundles.

Jeff took some photos while we waited. Looking at them later, I saw a father, smiling, exhausted but full of pride and devotion. And that father was me.

Ella and Maya were absolute angels on the flight. To help them with the change in air pressure, we gave them each a bottle on take-off and landing. I changed their diapers every two hours. The rest of the flight they slept peacefully. We received a lot of attention from both passengers and crew (who gave us just a bit of extra spoiling).

My thoughts also took flight, back to the birth mother, to Serena*. Just as I was thinking of her, at that moment, she was bound to be thinking of us.

Serena had informed our adoption agency, through her social worker that she wanted to meet us. The meeting took place in a quiet pizza restaurant in Chicago's South Side. Serena was accompanied by her adoption case worker, Janice*, who she spoke to nearly every day.

Jeff and I were early. We sat down in one of the booths so that we could have some privacy. We were terribly nervous. Then Janice came in, followed by a sturdily made African-American woman. She walked slowly, as if unsure. But then there was a flash of cosmic recognition, an invisible bond. Jeff and I leapt up, walked straight towards her, and what followed was a close embrace between soul mates that lasted for minutes. After we had sat down and ordered, there was a moment of silence. Then Serena asked: "Is it safe where you live?" My heart broke. I was able to reassure her. The second question came a moment later: "Do you have good schools?" Jeff and I happily told her about our lives, Brussels, Belgium. Serena said that she thought it was a good thing that Ella and Maya would grow up multilingual, that they would travel and see and learn things that she had never seen or learned. I asked her: "You do know that we are a gay couple?" Serena had to smile. She said that she had discussed this with her priest, and that he had had nothing against this, and neither did she. Janice told us how Serena had said "That's them" the minute she saw our photo album. And yes, there was a fantastic click between us. I loved this woman. We talked, Serena asked a lot of questions, told us that she loved reading, that it helped her get though sleepless nights. That she was a fan of the recently deceased Michael Jackson. I told her that I was an admirer of Diana Ross, who had discovered him. Serena was witty and lively, but her body and the look in her eyes betrayed the fact that her life had not been easy. After dinner, she asked if we could see each other again. We of course thought it would be good if we could answer any questions that our daughters might ask about their birth mother in the future. Then, all of a sudden, she said: "I want to thank you. You are my guardian angels." None of us could hold back our tears. This was the most moving thing that anyone had ever said to me. "No", said Jeff, "we should be thanking you, for trusting us." I had a deep respect for this woman. Everything showed that she was intelligent, sensitive and that she had made an excruciatingly difficult decision. She had also had the courage to share her sorrow with us, and this was a tremendous honor.

Yesterday, the day before our departure, Serena came to our apartment to say goodbye to Ella and Maya. She said: "I told myself 'This is not a goodbye – it is another Hello'". We left the three of them alone together. I heard her talking to them in a soft voice: "Hey Ladies, how you doing?" This was no simple, unstable woman. This was a *mother* who was dealing with her difficult decision as well as she could. Serena has a place in my heart for ever. She had an unbreakable bond with our daughters, and my only hope was that we could also forge just such a bond with her.

Landing at Brussels Airport in Zaventem with our daughters felt surreal. As if the dream had only then become reality. We were met by my parents and aunt Magda, as well as my brother and sister with their children. Everyone leaned over the baby carriers. 'They are so tiny!' By then they were almost 2.8 kilos. Ella and Maya had come a long way, but they were still dwarfed by their chairs.

We divided our luggage between the cars and drove home. Magda had decorated our house both inside and out. She had even found a poster of a black baby girl in a stroller with the text balloon 'It's a Girl!'

My lovely sister had bought changing tables and a heap of other stuff ("this should get you through the first three weeks").

We had a great brunch together, while our girls were cuddled incessantly. Then everyone left. Later, my best friend Tom and our best female friend, Raïssa came to see us (they are each going to be godparent to one of our daughters). I know Tom very well. He didn't say much, but I could see that he was very moved. Raïssa smiled and was very tender; then she told us the news that she was pregnant with her first child.

That evening, a strange peace descended on our house.

We were home, alone at last with our sweet, feisty little girls.

4 | A Contented House With Twins

4 September 2009
We had been asked by the municipal authorities to come and register our children.

Our girls were ten weeks old and growing fast.

We had decorated the children's room in the past month, even though the girls were still going to be sleeping in our room for a while. They were sleeping a little better each night.

Our family doctor was impressed; the girls had caught up well with regard to their weight and length. They were now within the curves for babies of their age.

My cousin Gevert, a talented photographer, came round to take portraits that we planned to use for a birth/adoption card for family and friends. The photos were beautiful: our two dark princesses were each in a blue robe on a white blanket. The cards were intended to satisfy the curiosity of acquaintances and to limit the number of visitors to close family and our best friends. Hectic schedules during the day made the girls restless at night. We received a flood of congratulations to our announcement. The most surprising reaction came from one of my uncles, who transferred a generous amount of money to the girls' account and explained in an emotional e-mail why he, as a heterosexual man, was so moved by what we were doing. My grandmother, who is eighty six, was determined to keep her end up and sent us a card with wise, deeply considered congratulations and reflections. I put the card away so that the girls could read it later – these are the things in family life that really matter.

We received a home visit from a *Kind en Gezin* (Child and Family) nurse, who had adopted her son from Brazil. We just clicked with Rita*, and she was to give us a wealth of advice and practical help over the next two and a half years.

During these first busy months, we also received regular help from a nurse from *Familiehulp* (Family Help). Arlette* was a sweet, calm older woman who was gentle with our girls, did the ironing and talked to us. She also had an adopted daughter and told us about the host of administrative obstacles that her family had had to overcome. I listened to her, but could not imagine having to wait three years, as she had done, before finally being allowed by a court to be the parent of my daughter in the eyes of the law.

We began looking around for a crèche. This was not an entirely simple task, as we wanted the girls to be in a Dutch-speaking environment, me being Flemish. One of the crèches I visited, with Maya in her carrier, was run by a woman who listened to my story, and said: "Your story touches me. My husband is originally from Burundi, he was also adopted. I will see what I can do". This angel phoned us back after a few weeks to say that our girls would be welcome in January. That was another weight off our shoulders. A year later, at the official opening of their new premises, the crèche's president of the Board came up to us: "I'm glad I've finally met you! I have heard so much about you and your daughters. Congratulations on your lovely family. We are so proud that you have chosen us!" And it proved to be a good choice; the team of devoted carers in this crèche gave our girls a wonderful time for the next two years.

During the first month we spent at home with our daughters we had our first appointment with Bonnie*, the American social worker who visits American adoptive families all over Europe as part of the next step in their adoption process. In the months that followed Bonnie was to help us comply with the formal requirements imposed by the court in Illinois. She had to write four reports, over four months, based on house visits, telephone interviews and our completed questionnaires. The questionnaires were comprehensive and covered everything from the children's motor development, eating habits and sleeping pattern, to questions about the parental roles within the family and dealing with difficult situations. We did our best to fill in everything as accurately as possible. On her first visit to our home, Bonnie stayed to lunch. She was a young blonde American with a soft expression and warm personality, married to a Dutchman and living in Amsterdam. She told us about the other families in the Netherlands, Germany and Belgium that she had brought into contact with each other through her tried and trusted *pot-luck* afternoons (all the guests bring a dish so that the host doesn't have to provide everything). She said she would also introduce us to a few other gay couples or fathers who had adopted one or more children from the United States. As she was leaving, she asked us if we could include a few extra photos of the girls in our reports. Bonnie had a "Wall of Fame" at home of all the adoption children she had guided during their placement, and she wanted a photo of our daughters as well. So typically American and sweet.

Down at the city hall, things were going less smoothly. The first time we had taken all our papers to the Registry of Births, Deaths, Marriages and Registered Partnerships, the official we needed to see was on holiday. We then received a message that the police would come to our house to check whether or not the girls were actually staying there, but then that was canceled. We now had a new appointment, this time with the right official. Once more, we dragged along a huge pile of paperwork.

At the Registry of Births, Deaths, Marriages and Registered Partnerships the official, who was extremely friendly, said that she had been in contact with the Inter-country Adoption Service of the (Belgian) Ministry of Justice (DIA). They had told her that our documents should be sent there. In the meantime, the municipal authorities could give us a "Declaration of Arrival", to prove that the girls were actually staying with us in Belgium. This was valid for three months. The ladies from the municipal registry congratulated us on our girls, and reassured us that they did not anticipate any problems with an adoption from a developed country like the US ("I mean, it's not like its Russia or Asia, is it?"). The director of the Registry of Births, Deaths, Marriages and Registered Partnerships promised that she would help us wherever possible.

Despite all these reassurances, I could not shake off a vague sense of unease.

Jeff was calm – after all, there is inevitably a pile of administrative paperwork in most countries – and sent off an e-mail to the Inter-country Adoption Service (DIA).

He gave a brief summary of the facts: he was an American who had adopted his twin daughters in Chicago, Illinois, USA under American law. He said that he had the court rulings to prove this and that he requested the cooperation of the various DIA departments concerned so that the children could be registered as soon as possible etcetera, etcetera.

9 *September* 2009
Today, we received an e-mail reply from a woman at the Inter-country Adoption Service (DIA). The message boiled down

to this:

All foreign adoptions must be submitted before the DIA in Belgium. In other words, a domestic American adoption must be submitted to them in Belgium if the adopting parents wanted it to be recognized in Belgium.

There was a form attached to the mail: "Application for recognition of an adoption conducted abroad", with a request to return the completed form. In small print at the bottom of the form it said "Adoption in a State NOT bound by the Hague Convention". I thought that this was rather strange; the US had ratified this international treaty on adoption on 1 April 2008, and Belgium had done so even earlier. During the next few weeks I checked this with two lawyers, but neither of them saw it as a problem "They probably only have one form for inter-country adoption" they said and "Oh, the official gave you the wrong form, that's their mistake."

We assumed it was just a minor detail. It turned out to be one which I should not have overlooked!

23 October 2009

We submitted all our documents to the Inter-country Adoption Service. We had been running around like madmen for the past six weeks, trying to get everything we needed for it. In the end we submitted a voluminous pile of papers; even more than we had been asked for.

It was an impressive package and I was proud that we had put together so much information for the authorities, especially as being parents was keeping us so busy. Jeff had been at home full-time for the past four months, while I was working part-time until the end of the year. I was traveling to Dusseldorf two days a week and working another half day at home.

But still, Jeff and I were so tired we were turning into zombies. The girls woke at around 6 am and had their final bottle around 11 pm (for the first six to eight weeks they were also fed at around 3 am). I learned to divide the day into zones of three or four hours and tried to take a nap in each one. In the mirror I saw the gray face with bags under the eyes of a middle aged man (until last June, Tom – my best friend – had always called me a *'faux jeune'*. Well, that was over, for sure).

We organized our days with the girls with the help of a wonderful, extremely practical book written by two British authors, one of whom is a doctor. *'A Contented House With Twins'* was to be our bible throughout and far beyond the girls' first year: the fixed structure and prescribed routine was good for all four of us, and helped our girls to become calm babies who ate and slept well.

It had been many years since Jeff and I had spent so much time at home in Brussels, and we really got to know our neighborhood and the people living in it again with a renewed curiosity.

To start off with, there were the neighbors across the street; an American couple with adopted African-American boys aged five and three. They had moved into an apartment opposite our house a year ago. We only knew them from the sushi restaurant further down the street. Now that we were always in Brussels and the girls were part of our lives, Raquel became a good friend; someone who knew all about adoption and trans-racial issues in a family – as well as knowing what it was like to have two small children in the house.

Later on we got to know a young couple from Limburg who lived further down the street. Their daughter was to go to the same crèche as Ella and Maya. Their cheerful attitude towards parenting and the warm welcome they gave our family meant that we soon felt a deep affection for them.

We also got more attention when we went out than we had ever had before. Shopkeepers got to know us, and some of our neighbors would stop us for a chat. Matongé [the African neighborhood in Brussels] is quite close to where we live, so occasionally we would get a curious look from an African, and sometimes someone would ask us "Are these your children?" We got the most comments from African women if we told them that the two warmly wrapped babies were *girls*. There would then follow an endless stream of tips and advice about how to make their black curls grow long and shiny. They could tell, no doubt, that there was no way these two white guys would ever be able to cope with the finer points of African hair care without their help. Each time this happened, I would resolve that when our girls were older, I would make sure they realized that they amounted to much more than their hair – be it straight, curly and with or without extensions.

4 November 2009

Today we received the first sign of life from the Inter-country Adoption service. They asked for an extra document: a copy of the passport stamps received when our daughters entered the country. This would be the only time they asked us for any extra information.

We were just happy to finally hear something from them, and

promptly sent them the scanned visa.

We had no idea then that this seemingly innocuous request was anything but innocent.

16 November 2009

Our dossier for acceptance of the adoption had been submitted three weeks ago and we were waiting impatiently for the DIA's answer.

Although Jeff was calm, I just could not relax. I contacted the lawyer who had accompanied us to the Flemish adoption officer. He said that it might still take a few weeks, but that he would make cautious inquiries into the state of affairs. After all, the DIA is apparently not known for either its quick work or its client-friendliness.

The lawyer promptly received a one-sentence e-mail in reply, stating that the case was in the workload of the official who had prepared it 'for signature'.

We had to be satisfied with that, so we concentrated on making the first vegetable meals for the girls. Jeff started to cook vegetables with the greatest care and devotion, pouring them into ice cube holders before putting them in the freezer. Maya and Ella loved all this new food from day one. We were so proud!

On the subject of cooking, our friend Raïssa, who was pregnant with her first child, proposed coming round once a week to cook for us. We were exhausted and this was an offer that we could not refuse. Raïssa is one of our dearest friends and we loved both her cooking and her company.

Today we left for the US to spend Christmas with Jeff's family. His parents have to go without seeing him for such long stretches throughout the year that Christmas is sacred. As usual we planned to return to Brussels straight after Christmas for New Year's Eve.

I planned the trip as if I was preparing for an Olympic event. It worked. A stewardess said to us: "You deserve an award for the way you've organized your trip! I love the zip-locs!" I had made a point of packing everything in separate plastic bags so that I would not have to rummage around in an over-full bag during the journey. So gay, as my straight friends would say.

In Zaventem, the check-in lady was surprised when we told her that we would be traveling to the US with the four of us from now on (she knew us from our former pre-daughter jet-set life).

Ella and Maya were real stars on the flight. They were calm, slept a lot and charmed the other passengers. They are so beautiful. Naturally, the cabin staff (especially the African-American stewardesses) wanted to hold and cuddle them. Normally I am against strangers taking such liberties, but I was willing to make an exception for these sweet, warm-hearted folks

We drove in our rental car from Atlanta to South-Carolina, to the village where Jeff's parents live. The family's US roots are actually in Pennsylvania, but they had moved south for work, 20 years earlier. As Catholic Northerners, they have remained outsiders among the Southerners, who are mostly evangelical Protestants and a lot more economically and socially conservative. But Mom and Dad's house and the area at the edge of a lake between the trees is wonderful. It is so perfectly quiet. On earlier trips we used to take the motor boat over the smooth water, or go fishing or swimming. Sometimes I would get up at six in the morning, put on my swimming trunks, jump into the inviting warm water and swim into the mists that hung over the lake like a soft, mysterious blanket. I loved our visits to the States!!

This holiday would be busier. Of course, everyone wanted to see the girls ("They're so big!"), there were dinners, shopping trips (the dollar was low), and we had family portraits made (special outfits for the girls).

No one can do Christmas like the Americans. Mom and Dad's house looked like something from a film set. There were miles of lighting: hanging in trees, along the roof gutter and down the walls. There was an entire menagerie of illuminated deer in the garden. A life-size Santa was climbing up the wall (hopefully, no one will think he is a thief and shoot him). A second Santa welcomed us with a song every time we came near the kitchen door.

It did me good to see Jeff so happy with his family — and so proud of our family!

Despite all this, I could not shake off a lingering feeling of unease. I didn't think that the scant information that we could squeeze out of the DIA about our dossier was normal and I didn't trust it. Jeff said that it was because of my background in Human Resources and communication (leadership, empathy, giving open feedback, etc.), but I wasn't convinced.

When we had asked the DIA again about how our case was getting on, we'd received a brief e-mail from the attaché who was supposed to be in charge of our dossier: "You will receive the decision by registered post once it has been signed." Jeff replied that we would be unable to receive any registered letters in December, as we would be on holiday in the United States. They did not reply to this. When our lawyer pressed them for an answer, we received another short message (by this time we were already in the US) saying, "The decision has been adjusted and is once more waiting for signature (....) we cannot give you any term for a decision."

We received a nicer e-mail on Christmas Eve: our adoption agency said that Serena, our daughter's birth mother, had been in contact with them and would really appreciate it if she could hear from us.

We phoned her, and once more I felt a wave of warmth and compassion for this woman and her sorrow, which had made our happiness possible. I thought her courage in seeking contact, despite her pain, to find out how the daughters she had said goodbye to were doing showed exceptional character. As agreed, we had been sending the adoption agency photos every month which they passed on to her. This would later slow down to one letter and photo album each year.

The adoption was to be pronounced final in Illinois next month, in mid-January. The four evaluation reports written by Bonnie had already been sent to Chicago.

4 January 2010
Back in Brussels.

Good news from the US: our lawyer in Chicago has told us that the adoption might be finalized on 20 January.

This was in total contrast to the situation in Belgium, where we had still had no news (and where we had not been able to establish residency for the girls). It was such a contrast that it spurred us both into action. We wrote an e-mail to the Minister of Justice, Stefaan De Clerck:

"Dear Minister,

I am writing to you for the following reasons.

[... we describe our adoption procedure ...]

I submitted a dossier [to the Inter-country Adoption Service] almost three months ago, containing all the requested documents (and more) with the required sworn translations and apostilles. In my accompanying letter [to the DIA] I also said that I was willing to answer any additional questions in my dossier. I think that it concerns a relatively simple case. [...]

Naturally, I am available to answer any questions you may have. [...]

Yours sincerely."

We never received an answer to this e-mail.

Two days later, I also sent an e-mail to the DIA. We told them that we were due to receive our adoption papers around the 20th of the month, and that we could provide a certified translation of them if required.

We received a short reply about five days later: "We will await [the adoption ruling] before taking a decision regarding your case." I was irritated by the enigmatic, hermetic and non-transparent manner of communication – it went against all my instincts and made me nervous. Meanwhile, it was time for the girls to start crèche. They were to go for three days a week. After spending six months caring for our daughters full-time, Jeff had gone back to work. He was going to work three days in the office in London and two days at home in Brussels. I said goodbye to my colleagues in Düsseldorf and went back to work at my employer's headquarters in Antwerp in a part-time position.

Ella and Maya were doing very well. The people at the crèche were taking very good care of them and taking note of everything, from their bowel movements to their motor and speech development. Maya was already looking around, wide-eyed, observing her environment curiously. Ella, with her angelic baby face, had finally grown her hair back (she had had a bit of cradle cap).

The adjustment went well for everyone, but Jeff missed us when he was away and it took me a while to get used to getting up three days a week at half-past five to get everything done by myself, and then coping by myself in the evening as well. Phew!

27 January 2010
I could not restrain myself.

I phoned Çavaria, the organization that champions the interests of LGBTs. I had read in the paper that the Flemish Minister of Welfare, Jo Vandeurzen, was organizing a Conference on Adoption and I wanted to know the position of the LGBT lobby.

It had been legal for LGBT couples to adopt for more than three years, but still not one couple had been able to adopt a child from abroad. So much for the law that had been introduced with such a fanfare!

This could not be right. The explanation of the Flemish adoption officer, if she was ever questioned about it, never went beyond vague sentences and shrouded statements. I should know – I had been following all her public communications very closely since our meeting with her, which was by now a year ago. My impression of her had not improved. Mainly she just confirmed my suspicions.

I did not hold back when I spoke to Çavaria. The position of Çavaria was not clear. When their spokesperson started beating around the bush I lost all patience and asked "What are you? Activists or subsidized civil servants?" (Later I thought that perhaps I should not have reacted so fiercely, as we needed them as allies.)

I sent another note to Çavaria, expressing my objections to the Flemish adoption officer's attitude to US adoptions. I, of course, had discovered what these were from our meeting with her, and from what she'd let slip during the conversation (she never made her position explicit in public). It seemed to me important that other adoption stakeholders knew of her attitude, as she was the public face of Flemish adoption policy, and she was not being honest. Her interpretation of the "subsidiarity principle" was misleading, to say the least: "Children may only be considered eligible for inter-country adoption if *all* possibilities in the country of origin have been *exhausted.*" This is not what the Hague Convention on Inter-country Adoption says: the Convention places *the child's best interests* first and foremost. According to the Treaty, every time there is a child in need it is necessary to find out what is in that child's best interests.

When the adoption officer had met with us, she had insinuated that the US had interpreted the Treaty "incorrectly" (her words) but this is just plain wrong. It is more correct to say that the US does not interpret the Treaty the way this adoption official would have liked it to. The adoption official continued to make this insinuation, without ever substantiating her arguments or revealing it in public.

Her general comments about adoption issues in the US were prejudiced to say the least. They gave the impression that she thought there was something potentially suspect about every adoption that took place in the US. What anyone should realize is that the US is a country with 50 states, each with its own family law and each with its own legislation on adoption. Adoption may look a little different in each of the States, but US federal law applies in every state, and this stipulates that the child's interests must come first and that a court must issue a ruling before any adoption may take place.

The Flemish adoption officer seemed inclined to invoke new rules for any case presented to her if she did not like the look of it. Her rules were not transparent and they were not communicated in advance. Her behavior raised the suspicion that she held ideological standpoints which she could not or dared not make public. She seemed to assess every application from prospective adoptive parents by her own criteria (I would receive confirmation of this from other contacts, and it seemed that a plan setting out fixed standard criteria for approving adoption channels did not even exist).

Quite simply, the Flemish adoption officer had a problem with the adoption of newborns in the US, as she believed that not enough efforts would have been made to look for other solutions, such as keeping the child with its biological family. This was yet another claim that she was never to substantiate (probably because it's not true!).

Finally, I told Çavaria my main arguments in favor of developing an adoption channel from the US to Belgium. Çavaria ought at least to know that an adoption channel with the US would also make inter-country adoption possible for the LGBT community.

One: the US has more than 500,000 children in all kinds of foster or institutional care. 100,000 of these children have parents whose parental rights have been terminated have been definitively dismissed from parental authority (therefore these children are eligible for adoption). However, many of them have very little chance of being adopted, as they have the 'wrong' skin color, a troubled background, they are too old, or they are brothers and sisters who cannot be separated.

Two: The US has ratified the Hague Convention on inter-country adoption. This entails the same guarantees for child protection as our own country. It is time that we treat the United States with the same respect that we show other signatory states to the Convention, particularly as the majority of inter-country adoptions in the Dutch speaking part of Belgium are from countries that have not even signed the Treaty.

Surely the above arguments were reason enough to enable a few dozen children to find a home here each year? And if a few of these children were found a home with parents of the same sex, so what?

Çavaria promised to keep me informed of their attendance at the Conference on Adoption, even if they did not hold out much hope for the outcome about adoption opportunities for LGBTs in Flemish Belgium.

It's enough to make you sick: the world is exploding with the misery of children who are suffering all over the world, but gay and lesbian couples here are not being allowed to give any of these children a loving home?

However, in our own world everything was going well. Our new-found friendships with a few couples who had also adopted African-American children were bringing our family a lot of joy. They were a mirror for Jeff and me, showing us that we were not alone. It made us so proud of our daughters (because of course, they will always be the most beautiful, have better manners, and be much more advanced than our friends' children). We were also closer than ever to our own families. My brother and sister both have children of around the same age as Ella and Maya, so our girls' extensive wardrobe can stay in the family for a while longer! My parents were pleasantly surprised by the dedication with which Jeff and I had approached parenthood. Sometimes I had the impression that when my father saw me taking care of the girls, he wondered if he had not missed too much of his children growing up. My grandmother, the mother of eight, was as proud as punch, and she clearly enjoyed our visits.

4 February 2010
Last week we received the final adoption papers from Chicago. Jeff was now definitively the legal father of our children. While we knew there was never going to be in issue with the Court in Chicago, we were ecstatic when we received the information.

I immediately sent the translated documents, with an original (including an apostille), to the DIA.

Our lawyer, Mr Deboutte, also wrote an accompanying e-mail:

"[...] These are the final adoption papers, irrevocably establishing the legal relationship between my client and his children. The wording is very clear. The court in Illinois has all the facts and has declared that it is competent. It furthermore rules that it is in the children's interest that they remain with my client. It is also clear [from the documents] that the children are eligible for adoption. My client has also been declared fit to adopt by the court in Illinois, and before that by the Juvenile Court in Brussels.

I consider that your decision must formally acknowledge this adoption: my client's dossier is transparent, and it must be clear from all the documents that this concerns a *bona fide* US adoption. [...]"

It was only after some prompting that our lawyer received the following e-mail: "Dear Sir, your client will be informed of our decision by means of a registered letter. If you request it in writing, we can also send you a copy of our decision." There was no mention of *when* this decision would be made.

In the meantime, Jeff and I had decided that we wanted to have our daughters baptized. We had been raised Catholic and we knew that the birth mother of our daughters was very religious. What's more, a baptism would give our girls entry to another community, that of our parish, where they could feel that they belonged. The priest at our church was very enthusiastic, and suggested holding the baptism during a Sunday service so that the entire congregation could be there. This was a great idea! We invited our parents, brother and sisters – in Belgium and the US – as well as our daughters' godparents, of course. Because our family has roots in both the US and Belgium, we had found godparents in both countries for Ella and Maya. I know that this might seem like too much of a good thing, but we wanted our daughters to know how wanted they are, and that there is somebody chosen for them by their fathers who they can trust in both parts of the world.

Then it was time to think about... the baptismal robes! They had to be stylish, but not old fashioned, chic but not too much, original, but suitable for a religious ceremony. As it turned out, we were so demanding (no news there) that we eventually had two baptismal robes made by a designer. Together with Raïssa, my best girlfriend, who works in Belgian fashion, we chose a beautiful roll of silk in Ghent, and we found the perfect model online for dresses that our girls would shine in. Ella's robe had a narrow top and a dress that billowed out like a ball gown. Maya had a dropped-waist dress edged with layers of lace! The dresses were so beautiful (not to mention quite expensive).

11 February 2010

I received an e-mail from the Çavaria spokesperson, giving me some feedback on our recent conversation. She confirmed that Çavaria may be invited to the Conference on Adoption, but said that as to whether or not they could actually influence the work group "that cannot be assumed. If none of our requests are included in the concluding text that will be sent to the minister, we will try to exert influence in other ways, or at least get some publicity for the case."

What could I say to that?

Our lawyer was also aware of the Conference, and told us that it is a closed circuit, composed of the "usual suspects": people from Kind en Gezin (Child and Family), the Centers for General Welfare Work (who conducts social service inspections of candidates), the adoption services and the Inter-country Adoption Service of the Ministry of Justice. All these working groups were led by a different professor of family law. I wondered how on earth this could produce a policy with a broad support base.

15 February 2010

Our lawyer e-mailed us. He had called the Head of Department of the DIA: the decision on our case would come this week. It was a matter of waiting. By this time, we had been waiting for almost four months.

Sometimes I couldn't sleep at night.

19 February 2010

Today we had been invited by the official at the Registry of Births, Deaths, Marriages and Registered Partnerships in our municipality. She had been trying to get our children registered in the foreign citizens register.

She was a warm woman. She told us that they had spoken to the DIA again, but had been told they had not yet made a decision on our case. Well, I guess it made a difference to hear it from someone else.

She had also contacted the Immigration Office, asking them to issue our children with a residency permit, because the DIA had been dragging their heels for so long.

In the meantime, she gave us a new Declaration of Arrival: a further temporary residence permit for the next three months.

5 | Fear

23 February 2010

A day I would never forget.

It was Tuesday, so I was due to work. Jeff was in London until the following evening. I got up at 5.30, prepared breakfast for the girls and ate some muesli, took a shower, put on a T-shirt and tracksuit bottoms, and gently woke the girls with some music. I dressed them both, then with one on each arm I took them downstairs to breakfast, hoping that there be no further pees or poops – every minute counts in the mornings. I sat them in front of the TV for a moment while I dressed in my suit and tied my tie. Girls in the car, briefcase, extra clothes for the crèche. By this time it was rush hour in Brussels and it took me quite a while to get to my office in Antwerp (Yet again I experienced a renewed respect for working mothers!). The day flew by and I was just in time to pick up Ella en Maya from the crèche.

Once at home I checked the day's e-mails. Among them was one from our lawyer with the title "refusal of recognition". I clicked to open it, but my hands and legs were shaking so much that I had to sit down. I could hardly breathe. I tried to read what the lawyer had written but I just couldn't. There was a sort of mist in front of my eyes and everything around me sounded as if it was very far away. I tried to stand a couple of times but my body was behaving like a rag doll. My heart seemed to be racing and standing still at the same time.

As soon as I could I rang Jeff. Whaaaaat?!

I translated the e-mail for him – with some difficulty as I was so wound up: "the reasoning behind this decision is as follows: the adopter (Jeff) effected the adoption in the United States by virtue of his American nationality, subsequently bringing the children to Belgium. He has done nothing to establish a legal framework for the adoption in Belgium and has acted with a complete disregard for Belgian adoption legislation. The adoption was *de facto* conducted with a view to evade Belgian adoption legislation, and in particular a number of regulations in the Civil Code."

What Jeff took from this was the fact that he was deemed to be guilty because he had entered into the adoption with fraudulent intentions. This was not the case, and as an American, it was hard for him to swallow the idea that he was seen as guilty by the Belgian state, without being able to even present his case or defend himself. Honorable Jeff, who was always so careful to do the right thing.

My main reaction was that my vague misgivings of the last few months had been justified – my instincts had not failed me.

The text of the e-mail was dry and its meaning was unmistakably clear.

What I did not realize at the time was that the events of this evening would awaken in me a raw power that I did not know I possessed.

It was the power of the unconditional love of a father for his children. A force was released in me which gave me the courage to do everything I needed to save our children and our family.

And along with this love there welled up a rage against anyone who said we were not allowed to be a family. That rage gave me the courage to batter down a thousand doors and ask for help from anyone who I thought might be able to give it.

This was going to be a battle. For life and death. For our family.

A short e-mail from the Inter-country Adoption Service: "With effect from the 23 February 2010, we do not recognize your adoption. This decision will also be sent to you by post."

I could have read it a thousand times and still not been able to believe it.

I had the entire text of the decision in front of me, but it was days before I could bring myself to read it. I simply could not make sense of the words. The style was too brutal to take everything in in one go.

The words in the decision of the Inter-country Adoption Service were like a stake through my heart.

In short, the adoption had been rejected for four reasons:

First: The Inter-country Adoption Service found that our adoption did not come under the Hague Convention on Inter-country Adoption because our preparatory course took place six months before the United States implemented the Convention in 2008. This despite the fact that our children were only born in June 2009 and that the adoption was only finalized months later in 2010, almost 2 years after the implementation of the Convention in the United States.

Second: The Inter-country Adoption Service found that the adoption could not be recognized because Jeff was, according to them, the only adoptive parent (Jeff is the only parent named in the documents), whereas the ruling on our suitability by Brussels explicitly stated that we were both deemed to be suitable to adopt. It was as though I had suddenly disappeared from the lives of Jeff and the children! This was nonsense. Of course the Inter-country Adoption Service were perfectly well aware that we had undertaken this project as a couple. Our entire case file expressed the fact that I, as Jeff's husband, was as much involved in this adoption project as Jeff from the very beginning. I was involved in the raising of these children as much as he was. I thought this argument was just plain wicked.

Third: The Inter-country Adoption Service found that Jeff had intended to deceive the Belgian state. This accusation was so unjust! How could they possibly come to such a decision without even having met us? Jeff is neither a fraudster nor a child-smuggler.

And fourth, the final straw, and what really shocked us: the Flemish adoption officer, from whom we had heard nothing for over a year, had apparently been only too happy to give her federal colleagues a helping hand with our case: "That she had met the adopter and his partner on 10 February 2009; that she had fully informed them of the problems with the United States of America as regards subsidiarity and the role of money in adoptions." What problems? As if adoption was a casual process in the United States, which failed to fully explore alternatives? And the "role of money" – without ever saying what was meant by that. This passage was also going to infuriate Jeff – as an upright American and adoptive father – because its deliberate vagueness was clearly intended to make our adoption look like some sort of child trafficking, condoned by the US government.

The hurtful manner of the Inter-country Adoption Service, ably abetted by their Flemish colleague the adoption official, would continue to haunt us.

Later, this same outrageous manner of the Inter-country Adoption Service would mean that we found help in many places; from civil servants, politicians and lobby groups, all of whom felt that nobody deserved to be treated that way. But of course we didn't know that at the time.

I immediately sent a plea for help to Çavaria:

"Our adoption is not recognized by the DIA.

[...] Jeff is being accused of trying to evade Belgian legislation. [...] We utterly refute this! Did the DIA really think that we, as two white gay men, would be able to 'smuggle' two little black babies into Belgium? [...]

As a gay couple, we stood little chance of adopting successfully in Belgium. [...]

We also utterly refuted the accusation that we were still trying to evade Belgian regulations."

I wanted to make sure that Çavaria understood that the Flemish adoption officer had had a hand in this and was involved in the Inter-country Adoption Service's arriving at a decision; Çavaria would also encounter her at meetings of the States General on Adoption.

Jeff contacted the American Embassy, and received a call back the same day. They didn't know what to do, but they promised to contact us again.

I made an appointment for myself with a well-known Member of our Federal Parliament of the Social Democrat Party.

[Note: Belgium is a federal state and has a multi party-system, with representatives of these parties mostly belonging to the Green Party, Social Democrats, Christian Democrats, Liberal Party and Flemish Nationalist Party. To establish governments on the Federal level and on the level of the Regions, these Parties form coalitions. By most international standards the above-mentioned parties could be considered belonging not far from the political center. Greens and Social Democrats are considered to be economically more left of center; the Liberal Party would be economically more right of center. The Christian Democrat party is

widely seen as belonging to the center economically and fiscally; while the Flemish Nationalist Party would be more to the right. On social and ethical issues, an important part of the constituency belonging to the Flemish Christian Democrats, is conservative]

He listened to our story, told me he happened to know that both the federal and Flemish ministers with responsibility for adoption were of the same political stripe and said: "This strikes me as a piece of political chicanery on the part of the Christian Democrats, but I advise you to challenge this decision in the Courts. There is a good chance that you will win, and in doing so you will help other couples." I was dismayed that this was the only solution he could suggest. Later, he was good enough to read the decision to refuse recognition himself and wrote the following to us: "The reasoning [of the Inter-country Adoption Service] is certainly brutal and actually quite shocking. In my opinion, the judge must demand evidence of the alleged 'intention to deceive'."

At least this was slightly encouraging.

A week later I went to see a well-known lawyer in Antwerp who specialized in immigration law. She said much the same: "Appeal the decision in court. There's a good chance that you will come before a judge who puts the interests of children before the objections of the Inter-country Adoption Service." As I left she told me that she was herself the mother of eight-year-old twin girls. Now I understood the warmth of her smile.

2 March 2010

Although I think our lawyer is a great guy, and also one who has important political connections, I was looking for extra ammunition to use against the opposition – the Belgian state (the Inter-country Adoption Service is after all part of the Ministry of Justice). It seemed clear to me that the decision of the DIA, which was arrived at with the 'help' of the Flemish adoption offi-cer, had something to do with the fact that we are two men.

I rang my good friend Sylvie, a lawyer in Leuven, to ask her advice.

I asked Sylvie whether she could think of a good lawyer who was part of the Leuven establishment – preferably somebody with links to the Catholic University *[The Catholic University of Leuven is the biggest university in Belgium, and very influential]*. We needed to find a mainstream lawyer of impeccable reputation; one who could both write and plead exceptionally well. Above all, we needed a lawyer well acquainted with the legal establish-ment in Brussels; one who carried a certain amount of authority in court. Sylvie gave me a couple of names. I rang Ms Vanden-berghe*. I made an appointment with her in just over a week's time.

Our appointment was for six o'clock in the evening. Three hours later Jeff and I were once more outside, completely ex-hausted and drained. In the next eighteen months I began to notice that this exhaustion happened each time we had to repeat our story (eventually I could no longer bring myself to tell the whole story and could barely do more than symbolically scream out my frustration. Jeff on the other hand would burst into tears almost every time our story was to be told by one of us).

Ms Vandenberghe looked just as impressively serious as I had hoped she would. She listened to our story. She made so many notes that I wondered if she wouldn't have been better entering it straight into the laptop, although I couldn't see one anywhere in her office. After listening for some time she said: "This is what comes of pushing through a law for which public opinion is not ready. And now we have adoption laws which have no public support." I was horrified by this; was I paranoid, or was she not in favor of same-sex adoption? I replied that I didn't think our problem lay with public opinion, but rather with the administration. I asked her if she was prepared to take the case. She replied "Yes of course, but we're a long way from winning it you know. I have no idea how I'm going to tackle it yet." As we left, I explained to her again that for us this was a matter of life and death, and that I really meant it. "I'd already realized that", was all she said.

In the meantime, our other lawyer, Mr Deboutte, had not been idle. He had contacted a couple of politicians who he thought might support us. He also contacted the Flemish adoption officer and the Cabinet of the Flemish Minister of Health: what was their position on our case? Was there any possibility of help from their quarter?

The reply of the Flemish adoption officer was brief: "[...] The situation you describe in your e-mail relates to a foreign adoption decision for which your clients seek recognition. This falls explicitly under the jurisdiction of the federal authorities [DIA] and is therefore not a case which can be dealt with at a Flemish level. There is therefore nothing I can do in this instance."

Well, well! As long as the decision of her federal colleagues was still to be made this official had no problem with helping them to come to a decision; but now that we were asking for her help, she suddenly had no authority with regard to recognition.

She had very properly cc'd the Cabinet of her Ministry on her e-mail. I could only hope that the Flemish Minister would be able to do something to help us.

After a couple of exhausting weeks – don't forget that with all this going on we still had to look after our beautiful daughters – we decided to take a weekend break in our London flat. I was a bit more stressed out about this then Jeff. What if we were arrested at the Eurostar check-in as a pair of child traffickers? Jeff begged me to stop this nonsense. As far as he was concerned this non-recognition was nothing more than an administrative nuisance caused by a few civil servants exceeding their brief.

By late afternoon I was getting everything ready for the trip. I took the opportunity to go through the post while Ella en Maya were having their afternoon nap.

My heart missed a beat when I saw the two envelopes addressed to our daughters – that is – addressed to the *birth name* of our daughters. I read the letter with shaking hands:

"To whom it may concern,

I have the honor to inform you that on 11 March 2010 the Public Guardian Mrs X has been designated in the capacity of Guardian to the Misses (Maya and Ella's birth name).

[…]"

I wanted to yell, my heart practically burst out of my chest, I felt dizzy. A guardian?!

They were going to come and take our children away. They would put them in an orphanage. They were endangering and humiliating our children by referring to them with a different name to the one on their passports. They wanted to destroy our family. We had to run away! How are we ever going to explain this to our children? Why were they doing this to our children? Why couldn't our children be allowed to have parents? *They were messing with our minds.*

I couldn't stand it. I had to tell Jeff. How could I tell Jeff? Could we still go to London? Were they going to stop us at the border? Were they going to charge Jeff with the abduction of our own children? Should we go and take refuge in the American embassy? Who could help us??

Somehow or other I managed to pack the bags and we caught the train to London. I was terrified that they would find our name in some sort of police register at passport control, but we were allowed through.

Once we had arrived at the flat in London we started to call people.

First we rang the American Embassy in Brussels (by this time it was Friday evening, and there was no one there who could help). I rang my brother-in-law Ruben, who is also a lawyer, but with a completely different specialty. I asked him if he had any idea what we could do. And we e-mailed our two adoption lawyers to ask whether they had expected this and what it meant.

Jeff and I discussed the situation. Jeff did not want to go back to Brussels if it meant that the girls might be taken away from us. (We later found out that under Belgian law that was entirely possible.) I didn't want to flee my own country as if I was some kind of criminal – that seemed almost like an admission of guilt. And how on earth were we ever going to explain this to our children? "Papa's country didn't think that you ought to be allowed to stay with us, so we had to run away."

Ms Vandenberghe got back to us with clear information which made me tremble with nausea:

"As regards the Public Guardian: the Public Guardian has full authority with regard to the children and also the right of custody and of decision-making as regards the fundamental options.

It is therefore the Public Guardian who may decide where the children are to live. [...] I would suggest that you contact the Public Guardian, who may well decide that the children may remain with you. As I see it, such a decision would certainly be in their best interests."

We learned from a well-placed source in Internal Affairs that minors would not be deported from Belgium. Small comfort.

Once again, I contacted the Cabinet of the Flemish Minister for Equal Opportunities, Pascal Smet, and spoke to one of their advisers, who promised to see if there was anything the Minister could do.

Jeff was also doing his share. He spoke for the first time to someone in the Office of Children's Issues in Washington DC. (This is a department of the American equivalent of the Foreign Office, the head of which, at the time, was Hillary Clinton.) The Office of Children's Issues looks after the interests of US minors abroad. The woman on the telephone ("Call me Jen*") had been alerted to the problem by the American Embassy in Brussels. She listened to our story and told us that she had never heard of a foreign Public Guardian claiming jurisdiction over an American minor. She promised to see what Children's Issues could do to help.

Jeff continued conversations with those "on duty" for emergencies at the US Embassy over the weekend. After all a foreign country had just taken custody of two American citizens. By doing so, the same country essentially stripped an American citizen of his parental rights.

I wrote yet another e-mail to Çavaria, explaining that a Guardian had been appointed and asking "What else can be done from your/our standpoint in this case? If there is nothing further that you can or will do, I would be grateful if you could tell me so and I will stop wasting both your energy and mine by bothering you with the problem."

There was no reply from Çavaria until after the weekend: "At this point, with all the information that we have, there is very little that can actually be done. Your example makes it perfectly clear – if nothing else – that the government must legislate on the question of adoption by same-sex couples so that this kind of dreadful situation need not occur. Our Political Working Group advises you to seek support from a diplomatic quarter. We suggest the American ambassador to Belgium ..." I nearly fell over.

We got through the days somehow or other, and returned without incident to our home in Brussels – although Jeff would rather we had all stayed in London.

24 March 2010

We received a disheartening mail from the American embassy. "Given the information that you have provided, we regret that we must inform you that the Embassy is not able to intercede on your behalf with the Belgian authorities."

Only a year later were we to understand that this reaction was the result of a sort of turf war which existed between the Embassy in Brussels and the Office of Children's Issues in Washington. The ambassador would have gladly taken the initiative, but he was prevented from doing so by the objections of the Office of Children's Issues, who preferred to handle the situation themselves. For this reason the Embassy had no choice but to send us their refusal.

The Office of Children's Issues continued to assure us, in the time that followed, that they were on the case and were developing the necessary initiatives.

We would come to suspect that Children's Issues definitely didn't welcome the interference of other services or of diplomats. The adoption which Jeff had entered into as an American in America had happened under the explicit guidelines of the State Department and the Office of Children's Issues, who regulated adoptions of this kind. A couple of months after our first contact with them, and as soon as Children's Issues had realized the actual circumstances of our case, they removed the guidelines which it had been possible to read online from the Internet, and replaced them with other information (ostensibly to prevent other Americans in Belgium , or anywhere else, from encountering the same problems). Our interpretation of their actions is that they were trying to cover up their own mistakes. Fortunately, we had always kept a couple of copies – a digital copy and a paper copy – of the information we had relied on and followed, and we were later able to confront Children's Issues with this.

But at the time we didn't know any of this, and so we were at a loss to understand the Embassy's unexpected refusal to help. Were the Embassy just going to drop us? We were puzzled, not least because the staff there had always been so friendly and understanding.

Jeff requested a meeting with the consul. It was to take place within the week. Jeff prepared notes, complete with 'discussion points' and a 'timeline' of events.

28 March 2010

This was the day that the guardian was coming to visit our children. She said she wanted to meet us.

At first Jeff simply didn't want to know. I had to persuade him that it would be best not to cross this woman.

She turned out to be pleasant, and with a soft voice, just as she was on the telephone. I wanted to trust her.

We showed her into the living room, where the girls were playing on their mat.

Then she explained that she wanted to get to know us, because it was her duty to establish that the children were safe (I tried not to roll my eyes). I said "Would you like to see where the girls sleep?" (Oh the humiliation.) No, that would not be necessary, she could see that everything was all right.

Then we said that we would like to explain a few things.

"Did you know that both girls have valid American passports, with Jeff's family name?"

Her reply was a rather surprised "No".

"Did you know that we have completed an American adoption process whereby Jeff is definitely now also the legal father of these children?" "No".

I wanted to ask her what she *had* thought in that case. Did she think she was ringing up to make an appointment to visit a couple of child traffickers? (I bit my tongue).

"This is all I received." She showed me a copy of our first interim court ruling, from July of the previous year, in which the judge in Illinois had made Jeff the girls' guardian. "I'm sorry, my colleagues told me that this was a very unusual case. I have never known an instance of an American child becoming the ward of the Belgian state. I had no idea that there had been an adoption. I would advise you to make an appointment to speak to my colleagues and explain the situation. I have no doubt that they haven't got all this information either. As far as I'm concerned I can tell you that I will do all I can to get this sorted out. I don't think that I have any part to play here, but do let me know if you think that there is anything I can do for you."

I explained to her that the girls still weren't registered as residents with the municipal authorities; that all we had was the Declaration of Arrival by way of a residence document, and that was actually only valid for three months. "Well," she said, "we can go to the Office of Immigration Issues and sort that out together."

We said goodbye to her. We didn't know what to think. Until today, this woman had had no idea that there had been a valid adoption process in the United States. She didn't know that the girls had valid US passports. And she seemed to be quite embarrassed about it. Was it possible that she could be on our side?

I look to Jeff. "I think that the DIA must have sent an incomplete dossier to the Public Guardian's office so that they would appoint a Guardian. And they did that precisely because it would be an extra blow for us."

"We'd better make sure our lawyers hear about this immediately", said Jeff grimly.

31 March 2010
Mr Deboutte had asked the Head of Department of the DIA – who would be our opponent in court – on what grounds it had been deemed necessary to appoint a guardian for our children.

The answer confirmed our suspicions. The DIA had never given the adoption papers to the Public Guardian's office. There was no way the Guardian could have known about the adoption.

The Head of Department referred to the legislative articles that stipulate the conditions under which a guardian may be appointed. One of the four mandatory conditions is that the child in question is not accompanied by someone who is their guardian or parent according to their country's legislation. But Jeff *is* their guardian!

The conclusion for us was that the legal conditions for appointing a guardian had not been met. Why was the DIA acting as if official documents from the US were just scraps of paper?

As if it mattered, the official from the DIA said that she had merely informed her colleagues at the Public Guardian's office: it was not she who had appointed the guardian, her colleagues at the Public Guardian's office had done that. Indeed they had ... because the DIA had made sure that they had not received all the relevant documents from the complete case file.

Mr Deboutte sent a brief reply: "Dear Madam, your answer is beyond belief."

The Head of Department had also written that the guardian had been appointed "in the children's best interests". Apparently it was fine to appoint a guardian "in the children's best interests" but those best interests could not be taken into account by recognizing their adoption. What hypocrisy!

Now I really wanted to arrange a meeting with the Public Guardian's Office.

23 *April* 2010

I didn't know what to expect from our appointment with the

Public Guardian's Office. Until recently, I had not even known of its existence.

We were shown into an area which was a cross between an empty office, a storage space and a junk room. In the middle were a small table and a few chairs. A few minutes later, a young blonde man came in. He had a West-Flemish accent and did not really look like a civil servant, more like an inexperienced kid. He had our case file with him, looked very much at ease and was very friendly.

He listened to us patiently.

And then it came. "To be entirely honest with you, we are feeling rather used by our colleagues [at the DIA], who did not even provide us with a complete case file. You have nothing to fear from us: on the contrary, we think that we can help you with the correct residency papers for the children for the duration of your court case. We also propose that our guardian make a statement before the court, possibly in writing, saying that it is in the children's interest to have the adoption recognized. We are also going to declare that our department has assessed you and that in our opinion you are in the best position both materially and emotionally to raise the children. Ask your lawyers what they think of this. Anyway, once you have a residency permit, if your lawyers think that it would give you a better chance in court we will see if we can terminate the guardianship immediately. We think that there is some kind of political game going on in your case and we don't want anything to do with it. Please keep us informed of all future developments and do not hesitate to call on us for help for as long as we are involved."

I was so happy that I could have jumped up and kissed him (I managed to control myself). But what I thought was even better was the fact that he had said, without any prompting, that they thought that politics were playing a role in our case.

Jeff was finally able to believe that the Public Guardian's Office was not going to take our children away from us. A small drop of relief in a sea of sorrow and humiliation. Jeff brought the Embassy and the US Office for Children's Issues up to date on developments. We had heard nothing from them for the past few weeks other than that "talks were taking place at the right level". How enigmatic and opaque can you be?

In the meantime, our other lawyer, Ms Vandenberghe, was drawing up a synthesis of her version of the petition and that of her colleague Mr Deboutte (we wanted our lawyers to work together, each with their own particular strengths). With angelic patience she incorporated my comments, or if she did not want to do this, explained why it would be better not to put some of these points into the petition. I thought that she was doing a great job, and I was glad that she was on board.

To distract us, there was the first fitting of the baptismal robes. They were going to be fabulous! Ella and Maya would look even more beautiful than usual. More good news: Jeff's brother Russ and his family, and another one of Jeff's nephews would be at the baptismal celebration. They were planning to base a European trip (London, Paris, Brussels and Bruges) around it. Jeff was so pleased about this, and I was happy for him. We were going to have all of them and Jeff's parents to stay. With seven guests and the four of us, it was going to be a full house! Jeff had not told anyone in his family about our 'administrative' problems in Belgium. He did not want to worry his parents by telling them something that they could do nothing about. He was right.

My brother, sister and parents did know about the problems. My brother and sister were giving me the support I so badly needed. But I had regretted sharing our problems with my father. Sometimes I saw the sadness in his eyes (I think he was worried that his granddaughters might be deported). I also did not want his sadness to become part of his relationship with his granddaughters. Their relationship should be the open, carefree bond that every grandparent and grandchild is entitled to.

6 May 2010

Today we had an appointment to go with our daughters' *guardian* – I could still hardly bear to say the word – to the Office of Immigration Issues to see about arranging a residency permit.

We met at North Station, within walking distance of the Office of Immigration Issues. I was not familiar with the neighborhood. The building was a brown sky scraper, foreigners were walking around both inside and out: people on their own; people who looked as if they had nothing; families with children — dressed too warmly for this time of year. Nearly all of them were black or brown.

The guardian said "most of the children under my guardianship either come from war-torn areas or they are Roma."

I was overwhelmed by what I saw. A man was kicking up a fuss at the reception desk, it looked like a scene from a film.

We were allowed to take the lift upstairs immediately, and were shown into the office of the official who was dealing with our case. It was a young woman with a nice face, warm personality and an East-Flemish accent.

She listened, said she had never heard of a problem concerning an American before and explained the possibilities. On the basis of a circular letter, two Declarations of Arrival would be issued to *non-accompanied minors* (I had to bite my tongue at this point), followed by a temporary permit that would be extended after a specified period.

We showed her the adoption papers and the girls' passports.

I asked, nervously, in what name the residence documents would be drawn up. (I couldn't bear the way the Inter-country Adoption Service always used the girls' birth name instead of the names on their passport. This could lead to a lot of confusion – an identity crisis even – when they were older, couldn't it? Didn't the IAS realize this? Of course not. This behavior of theirs also had a racist side to it for me. When people were taken as slaves in the US Colonial Period, the first thing they lost was their own name. They then took whatever name their owner wanted to give to them. It was inhumane and humiliating then, as it was now.)

What she said made our day: "The children have valid American passports. Residence permits are always issued on the basis of valid proofs of identity."

6 | Waiting, writing, hoping

27 May 2010

Today I attended the Closing Seminar of the Conference on Adoption, organized by the Flemish adoption Officer. It was being held to present the outcomes of the various working groups on adoption and sum up the conclusions on which the new decree would be based.

A few things shocked me.

First of all, parents of adopted children were nowhere to be seen. Surely they are well placed to provide information that could help shape the new policy?

There was some testimony from people who had been adopted and who had set up a help group. But where were the accounts of adoptions with a happy ending? Why were there no adoptees who could talk about their roots without shame or unprocessed grief? Weren't we allowed to hear their stories? Are positive stories about adoption at odds with the policy our government wants to promote?

After the testimonies, it was time to hear from the chairpersons of the working groups; all professors of family law. One of them talked continuously about special needs adoption parents (meaning LGBTs who may be eligible to adopt), and special needs children (those with heavier emotional or physical baggage). The tone suggested that there is no place for either in Flanders. It was so incredibly rude. What a slap in the face for all the many committed parents – gay and straight – who have no objection to adopting a child with a difficult background! And what a message to be sending out to children who need extra care, whether or not they are adopted. "Sorry kids, but we'd rather not have you!"

The speaker from the Institution of the Hague Convention on Adoption, gave a rather discouraging speech. I remember him saying "Many consider us a nuisance, but if we were not here, there might be no inter-country adoptions at all". I thought it was strange for a man speaking on behalf of a Convention that attempts to protect children, one which commands member states to act purely in the interests of the child, to display such a negative attitude towards inter-country adoption.

And then, to cap it all, the host of the conference, the Flemish adoption officer, just said "a few words in passing" in a speech of less than ten minutes. Instead of clearly setting out her vision, she muttered a few vague terms about 'problems', 'obstacles' and 'waiting lists'; no policy statement, strategy, priorities, action plan – nothing. She left any further speech making to her minister, Vandeurzen, (who simply announced that a new adoption decree was coming). I thought it just wasn't good enough. Why does Flanders have an Adoption Officer who is either unable or unwilling to tell the public what she stands for?

I walked home feeling sad. Imagine my daughters had been sixteen and I'd taken them to this conference. I would have been mortified. What would adopted children think about themselves and their identity if they saw something like this? Adoption had been referred to in nothing but negative terms all day. Why can't those in Flanders acknowledge that adoption is fully acceptable as an alternative way to make a family; a process that can benefit everyone in the adoption triangle in the long-term? Instead of trying to hush up the problems, wouldn't it be better to face the challenges, and tackle them with the sort of positive vision which other governments express? Wouldn't it be better if adoptive parents and their children could count on a government who would help and support them in the specific challenges they face?

It had all got too much for me. The accumulated stress of the past few months could no longer be suppressed. I was exhausted by our efforts to spare our children these problems. Next day at work Yvette, who had been my assistant for years and who has also become a good friend, listened to my story. I could not hold back my tears any longer. Yvette walked to the door of my office, closed it, stood in front of my desk and looked straight at me with a piercing stare (you wouldn't want to be in her bad books): "Lieven, listen to me. Everything will be all right, because it HAS TO BE all right, OK? Keep strong, do everything you think you have to do to arrange this and don't be put off by a bunch of frustrated civil servants who see you as a scapegoat that they can pick on to abuse their power. Concentrate on your children and on making them happy. You are wonderful with them, they could not be better off anywhere else. Everything will be all right! And now get back to work!" Now that's Yvette for you.

Two days later I received a long e-mail from her. She expressed her sympathy for us and reminded me that I could tell her anything, that she cared for us and that we are good fathers to the children. I will keep and cherish this e-mail and I am eternally grateful to Yvette for her unconditional friendship.

13 June 2010

The day of our daughters' baptism! Our house was full of guests – Jeff's parents, his nephew Connor, brother Russ, sister-in-law Kathy and their two daughters Courtney and Amanda. Our friend Bobby from Washington DC also came for the weekend, and Stephanie, another friend, came from London with her husband and son.

Our American guests and Belgian family and friends met up at the church. Almost everyone already knew each other from parties, visits or weddings.

Our daughters looked stunning in their silk couture dresses. They were adorable. Recently little Ella has shot past her sister in length. And she has big feet, so cute! Ella is tall and slender, while her sister is more compactly built. Maya started walking at eleven months. Both babbled incessantly (they still do). Sometime they had conversations with each other (goodness knows what about) and they could also wave hello and goodbye. They clapped their hands when they were excited about something. And yes, they were the sunniest, most beautiful and smartest daughters we could wish for!

During the ceremony, Johnny, the priest, who knew all about our story, spoke wise, kind words. He said that the girls were each named after an African-American icon. Their second name (after their grandmothers) expressed their new identities, while their third name (the name they were given by their birth mother) expressed their roots. Johnny explained how the girls had come into our family and praised their birth mother, a religious and dignified woman who wanted the best for her daughters.

Jeff and I also said a few emotional words and thanked our family, the godparents and the people from our parish.

Afterwards we went to eat with family and friends in a friend's restaurant. He had kept it open especially for us. It was a lovely afternoon and everyone enjoyed themselves.

14 June 2010

Today our lawyer, Ms Vandenberghe, was attending the initial hearing of our case. She was going to try to agree on a time limit for submitting the statements (written word and reply between the parties) so that our case could be dealt with before the end of the year.

Everything was taking so long! It would be months before we could even see a judge. When Jeff heard that we would have to wait seven months for the hearing his exasperated reaction had been "What kind of idiotic country is this?" I had to admit he was right. All the waiting around, not being able to do anything, was driving me mad as well.

Despite all our problems Jeff somehow found the time and energy to look for another job. He was so good at selling himself that he was offered two jobs and had the luxury of choice. Jeff is incredible. There is no way that I could have done that during this period.

I received another mail from one of Minister Pascal Smet's officials saying he would be speaking to someone from Minister Vandeurzen's cabinet at the beginning of next month. I hardly dared to hope for anything.

12 July 2010

We went to the seaside for a week at the invitation of my sister and brother-in-law, who have two daughters. We stayed in a chalet on a leisure park. Not exactly my type of holiday, but it was easy and there was a huge tropical water paradise where our daughters could enjoy all kinds of watery fun.

The days were quiet and pleasant and revolved around the

four children. In the evenings the adults could relax and enjoy a bottle of wine with dinner.

One day, we met a family who had adopted two girls from Ethiopia. They asked us for tips on how to take care of their daughters' hair (because of course after all the advice we'd had our girls' hair was in perfect condition).

The week at the seaside had reminded Jeff of his childhood, so we decided to go to Rehoboth Beach in Delaware, on the east coast of the US, in September. Rehoboth is a three hour drive from Washington DC and Jeff spent a lot of holidays there with his parents as a child. We had also been there together a few times. It is a small, cozy seaside town that never gets too busy. It has a few nice antique shops and good restaurants, and it's a world away from the noisy seaside towns that you often find in the US. It is frequented by a mix of working class families from the neighboring States (Pennsylvania, Maryland, Virginia) and more affluent, urban professionals and LGBTs from Washington DC. It would be our first time there with the girls and I was looking forward to it. As we would be flying to the US capital we would also be able to visit friends there.

By now, Jeff's armor was also beginning to crack. Living with this level of uncertainty about our family for so long, and not knowing how things were going to turn out was also beginning to weigh heavily on him. I could see the tension in his face.

He wrote a strongly worded letter to the US ambassador in Brussels and sent copies by registered post to everyone in the Embassy and the Office of Children's Issues with whom we'd had contact. It had been three months since we had heard from either agency.

His letter to the ambassador said: "I understand that the US must operate under certain restrictions with regard to foreign countries. Nevertheless, do the Embassy and the [American] State Department tolerate the fact that the Belgian State does not respect the fundamental rights of my children, who are American citizens? Will the State Department stand by while a foreign state assumes legal guardianship of American children, overriding the rights of their legal parent, who is also an American citizen? Does the State Department not consider the above to be in violation of international treaties (The Hague Convention on Adoption, European and UN conventions on the Rights of the Child, and Conventions on Human Rights)?"

Jeff does have a fierce side, which he doesn't often demonstrate and which I really admire.

I guess I don't have to repeat that the situation was really getting the best of me sometimes?

We already had our hands full taking care of our darling daughters. The constant worry, the sleepless nights, trying to devise solutions that were never found, work – it all took its toll. I sometimes heard or saw myself and was shocked that I could no longer recognize the cheerful, optimistic person I had always been. Instead, here was somebody who couldn't express his anger and frustration, and who was bottling it up dangerously inside.

I made an appointment with my family doctor, a no-nonsense type who had known me for a long time. I wanted her to send me to a therapist. That way I could pay someone to listen to my outpourings of anger, and it would weigh less heavily on me the rest of the time.

She listened to me and said: "Lieven, there is nothing wrong with you. Your anger and feelings of powerlessness sound like the normal coping mechanism of a healthy mind. Don't you enjoy a sport that might help you to vent your anger? Swimming is healthy, and you could hit the water. Or you could buy a boxing ball to attack when the going gets tough."

I took her advice.

The doctor also suggested seeing me more often. I had no symptoms of illness – no signs of depression or other disorders – but she had done some courses on wellbeing and psychology, and thought she might be able to help me. We agreed that we could stop this process at any time if either of us felt uncomfortable with it.

So I went to see her faithfully every two weeks for the next year, to cry, rage, fulminate or just tell her what wonderful daughters I had the privilege of raising.

3 *August* 2010

Apparently our registered letter had reached the ambassador. He sent an e-mail saying that he had started to ask questions about our case and would get back to us as soon as possible. He wished us all the best.

Soon after this we received another mail from Jen, our contact person at the Office of Children's Issues in the US. The tone of this e-mail was more stand-offish:

"[As a result of your case] we have developed guidelines for all prospective adoptive parents [from the US] living abroad. We have made this information available on our website: [...].

Nevertheless, we have asked [the Belgian inter-Country Adoption Service] about the legal options available for adopted children who, [...] like your children, were adopted in a domestic US adoption. I am waiting for an answer from the Belgians.

In the meantime, it would be helpful to know how far advanced your case is in Belgium. What legal strategy is your Belgian lawyer following? [...]"

We were shocked: it seemed that when the Office of Children's Issues had realized that American citizens were getting into trouble for following their guidelines they had quickly changed the rules. They seemed uninterested in the fact that both we and our lawyers in Belgium and the US had acted on this information in good faith. There were no apologies, no attempt to explain to the Belgian authorities that the American citizens who were now encountering problems in Belgium had followed US guidelines.

The Office seemed to be more concerned about their relationship with their foreign counterparts than the welfare of their own citizens.

The new link on the State Department's website to information for prospective adoption parents was certainly more low-key with regard to the opportunity for American citizens to adopt in the US if they were living abroad.

Obviously, this was no help to us.

As the Office of Children's Issues and the Embassy had both asked us to be sure to keep them meticulously up-to-date, I started translating all our correspondence with the Belgian DIA into English.

Jeff wrote a long e-mail containing a time line of the events and a translation of our petition to the court. He also provided some extra information that we thought the Americans should definitely be made aware of:

First: the DIA had never asked to see or speak to us, either before or after they made their decision. They had not communicated their decision until four months after they had received our case file. If they did believe that Jeff had circumvented Belgian law, why didn't they inform the US authorities, or even the embassy? After all, we had concealed nothing from them. If they had wanted to they could even have phoned the adoption agency in Chicago to ask them to stop the American procedure!

Second: we reiterated the point that the DIA had been in possession of our case file for two weeks before they had informed the Public Guardian's Office that we might have two "unaccompanied minors" living with us (this solved the mystery of why they wanted a copy of the girls' visa). But the DIA had then waited another three and a half months before informing us of their decision. This flies in the face of any principle of transparency. Leaving us in the dark about a development which would have such major consequences for our lives also demonstrated an utter lack of integrity.

Third: their argument that it was impossible to reverse the refusal to recognize the adoption because a court case was pending was simply untrue. The Minister of Justice, De Clerck, has the power to review his administration's decisions. Unfortunately, we had received no response to any of our attempts to contact him.

Fourth: The Flemish adoption officer has the authority to investigate and approve the adoption channel that we had used (the adoption service in Chicago). There was nothing by way of an act or decree that would have prevented her from doing so. Her superior, the Flemish Minister for Welfare, was also authorized to do so. Unfortunately, no one from his cabinet had ever responded to our questions.

Fifth: a particularly humiliating fact for our children is that the DIA refused to use the names on their passports, and consistently used their birth name. There was no legal grounds for using their birth name as this name did not appear on a single legal document. We already knew that their Belgian residence permits would be issued in Jeff's name, therefore, it seemed that the DIA persisted in using the birth name purely to make a point, with no regard as to how this might affect our children.

Finally: Jeff had acted in good faith as a citizen of the United States. This adoption was a kind and decent act. Now he was at the mercy of government officials who were accusing him of "deception" and "attempting to circumvent Belgian law". He found this very hard to bear, and was deeply upset about the need to clear his name in court.

16 August 2010

Today our lawyers sent us the first statements from the opposing party, the Belgian DIA. They made me so sick that I could not read them all in one go. I knew that I would have to translate it all into English for Jeff and listen to his reaction. My pain would be doubled.

One paragraph in the DIA's argument really stuck out: "... although theoretically the legal opportunity exists for LGBTs to engage in inter-country adoption, in practice this opportunity is virtually non-existent. Most countries of origin consistently prefer heterosexual couples."

This was the first time that the DIA had actually referred to our sexuality in black and white. They also quoted information from the confidential meeting that we had had one and a half years prior with the Flemish Adoption Officer. Confidential for us that is; apparently not so confidential for her.

The allegation that straight couples are preferred to gay and lesbian couples has no legal basis, as this is not an issue in the state of Illinois.

Even after everything that had happened I had not expected the opposing party to be so crude.

The thing that got to Jeff most were the insinuations about "problems with the United States in connection with subsidiarity [in adoptions] and the role of money [in US adoption]." This could only have been intended to relegate our adoption to some kind of shady gray area. It even seems to imply that we might have *bought* our children. This was almost more than Jeff could bear. The costs involved in adopting our two girls had been less than the fees it would cost a Belgian parent to bring just one child from Asia. We could have told the DIA that if they had even bothered to ask us.

And what about the interests of the children? Should that not come first? The US decision on our adoption refers explicitly to the interests of the children, which was the basis of our adoption. But the DIA just set this decision aside: "The [DIA] is authorized to judge whether the adoption of a child was in the child's best interests at the time of adoption and not at the time of the assessment. It is therefore not authorized to assess whether or not recognition is in the interests of the child."

So the DIA had no authority to take our children's best interests into account when deciding whether or not to recognize their adoption. And they were hereby absolving themselves of all blame. What happened to the children as a result of their refusal to recognize the adoption was not their problem — it was up to the Public Guardian to sort that one out!

It felt as if the inmates had taken over the asylum.

I managed to translate all this, and Jeff sent it on to the US ambassador and the Office of Children's Issues at the State Department.

Three days later we received a message from the ambassador: "I cannot intervene in a legal discussion or a court case. I will consider this matter and discuss all the diplomatic options."

The Office of Children's Issues did not even reply.

26 August 2010

Jeff was saying goodbye to the colleagues in his London office and I was with him. He had invited them for a drink in the restaurant on the ground floor of the building in Canary Wharf. Docklands is a soulless neighborhood where the hordes of skyscrapers housing major banks are encircled by the council estates of the east end of London.

It did me good to see Jeff being praised to the skies by the people he had worked with for the past six years.

In true London style it was not long before everyone had had one drink too many, and it was a fun evening.

Everyone asked us how our daughters were getting on. I was feeling pretty downhearted, but I tried to give a cheerful account of their latest antics and their first words, and joined in discussions on whether twins are easier or more difficult to raise than siblings of different ages.

Thank goodness we would be going to the States next week. Holiday!

3 September 2010

We settled into our hotel near Dupont Circle in Washington DC. As a large chain hotel, it was the kind of place we would have avoided like the plague in the past, but now we had chosen it for the very factors we used to turn our noses up at. It had practical rooms with large beds, a free bar and buffet between five and seven pm (Who on earth eats so early? We do!). They are used to customer requests at this hotel, so there was no problem when we asked for two children's beds.

Several of our friends in the area had invited us to stay with them, but our daughters were still so young that we did not feel at ease everywhere.

One couple of friends, Ed and Michael, really took our breath away. They have a house in Arlington, just outside DC, in the state of Virginia. They had just given their DC *pied-à-terre* a makeover. They were proudly showing us around when they said "We've made a few adjustments so that all four of you can stay here in future!" And indeed, the bottom floor had been turned into a large two-room flat for guests, with a separate bathroom and television corner. It was beautifully done, very stylish, with lots of glass and white walls, *European Style* (which means it looked typically American).

Ed and Jeff have been friends for twenty-five years and Ed was a witness at our wedding. Although we only see each other once or twice a year, we always just pick up where we left off. They are two wonderful friends.

By this time, they knew about our situation. They asked us whether we had considered telling our story to the American press.

Ed is a lobbyist with an enormous network on Capitol Hill.

He is a familiar face at all kinds of political lobbying parties, where he often meets political journalists. Michael is a psychotherapist, whose practices in DC and LA serve a host of celebrity clients who come to him for transformation and crisis intervention (unfortunately he is not allowed to tell us any juicy details about them). He too has access to top journalists.

They suggested contacting a journalist at the Washington Post, as they were sure that he would publish our story if we gave our permission. There were also possibilities at CNN and maybe Oprah Winfrey's company.

Ed and Michael suggested framing the story and highlighting a number of the elements that could work well in the US press: the differences in attitudes to adoption between the US and Belgium ("a country which hasn't even got a government", sniffed Ed – which happened to be true at the time), the discrimination element ('liberal' Europe, which actually discriminates harder against gays than the US when you get right down to it), and the racial aspect (black twins from Obama's city of Chicago who aren't allowed to be adopted by a US citizen living in Belgium).

It was a very kind gesture, and I was grateful to them for being prepared to put their network at our disposal. It was true that in our despair we had considered making our story public — we had already been approached a few times in Belgium — but what good would it do us? And more important: what impact would it have on our children? Jeff and I were to discuss this many more times in the future.

We spent the second week of the holiday in Rehoboth Beach, Delaware, where each day our girls ate their quota of sand. They loved it, and they also enjoyed the attention of the many friendly Americans who came up to talk to us.

The return journey to Belgium went without a hitch. The girls behaved perfectly and I was beginning to wonder if those stressed out parents with naughty children on planes didn't have only themselves to thank for their problems.

27 September 2010

We still hadn't heard anything from the Office of Children's Issues since writing to them a month before, so Jeff sent another e-mail asking whether they had any news.

We promptly received a long e-mail in which our contact person, Jen, explained that there had been both correspondence and a telephone conversation between them and the Belgian DIA. For the first time we were shown some of the e-mail correspondence (I thought it was peculiar that the names of the contact persons from both sides had been blacked out). During the telephone conversation, the DIA had apparently confirmed to their American colleagues that the only legal route available to us was the one we were already following: taking the Belgian State to court.

But were Children's Issues prepared to just accept the Belgian explanation?

Jeff sent a long e-mail back explaining matters in even more precise detail. We felt that there was not much progress and, more importantly, that the talks aimed at finding a solution were not happening between the right people.

We emphasized that a long legal battle was not the only option. The DIA could simply review their earlier decision in the light of everything that had been revealed since its refusal to recognize the adoption. It could also ask its Flemish colleague, the adoption official, to approve our adoption channel with retroactive effect, or urge its Flemish colleague to approve our channel for the future and give us the opportunity to adopt the children again in the US, in accordance with Belgian requirements.

We thought that there were three main reasons why the DIA had refused to consider any of these options; reasons that were now becoming obvious.

There was the negative attitude of the Flemish adoption officer and her Federal colleagues at the DIA to adoptions in the US.

They continued to allege, without any proof, that people "paid" for children in the US.

The DIA and the Flemish adoption officer had no problem with putting into writing that, theoretically, there were legal opportunities for LGBTs to adopt children, but that it wasn't really possible in practice. In other words, the law does not discriminate, but the civil servants do. Well that means that the legislation is meaningless and may as well not exist!

It was as clear as day, we wrote, that political machinations way above our heads were involved here.

It was also the first time that we dared to tell the Office of Children's Issues that we found it unacceptable that they had still not written an official letter to the Belgian authorities, and that apparently no political or diplomatic discussions had been conducted on the matter. US citizens would just have to accept that if they went to live abroad they might risk losing their adopted children to a foreign state without any hope of a solution. What on earth had to happen before the Office of Children's Issues would finally take action?

It was a long time before we received an answer to this e-mail.

We received the draft of our lawyers' final brief before facing the opposing party in court. It contained our final arguments against the DIA and their refusal to recognize our adoption.

Our lawyers had done their work well. They had distilled our emotional stories and loaded discussion into a dry, well-substantiated and crystal clear discourse. Ms Vandenberghe, who had at first seemed rather cautious about taking our case, had really immersed herself in it and was now as infuriated by the attitudes and practices of the DIA as we were.

The DIA continued to allege that our adoption could not fall under the Hague Convention on Adoption as our *preparation course* had taken place four months before the US had ratified the Adoption Covenant.

Our lawyers argued that this was nonsense. Following a course is not the same as adopting a child. The Hague Convention was in effect in the US (it had been so since April 2008) at the time of the adoption procedure (from July 2009 until January 2010). That was plain fact. Therefore the principles regarding the protection of children, as guaranteed in the Convention, had been respected.

Our lawyers also refuted the DIA's insinuation that standards for assessing adoptions were lower in the US than in Belgium. This was manifestly incorrect and the DIA had never provided any proof of this, only false accusations.

If the adoption fell under the Convention, it must be recognized in Belgium by operation of law.

What's more, the DIA claimed that we had filled in the wrong "application for recognition" form: we had filled in a form for a *Non Hague* adoption, and therefore the recognition could not be a Hague recognition. But we had simply filled in the form they had sent us. Our lawyers made short shrift of this pathetic, formalistic argument: you can't send people the wrong form (possibly on purpose) and then blame them for not filling in the right form (It was strange that I had already noticed that maneuver at the very first beginnings of contacts with the DIA).

Our lawyers had even devised more arguments, just in case the court ruled that the adoption was not a Hague inter-country adoption and therefore subject to different rules.

They rejected the other party's argument that the adoption could not be recognized because Jeff was the only person "carrying" our adoption project, while the papers from Brussels stating that we were fit to adopt had named *both* of us. Our lawyers maintained that all facts and documents demonstrated that we had both been equally involved in this adoption project from the very beginning, and that I was also raising the children in an equal capacity. *Of course* we were committed to this project as a couple. Furthermore, we were married and lived at the same address, we had appeared together in court in Brussels and Illinois, my name was also on court documents and on the post-placement reports that Bonnie had written.

Our lawyers also remarked that it was the Flemish adoption officer who was refusing to conduct a serious investigation into channels with the US and who continued to hide behind allegations regarding the "lack of subsidiarity" and the "role played by money" in US adoptions. They pointed out that our adoption had been organized by a not-for-profit organization, and one which does not offer adoption as the only solution to mothers in need, but that examines *all* possible options for families in need of help. Our lawyers also explained the high level of transparency required by the court in Illinois regarding adoption costs. The insinuation that money had played any role in our adoption was complete nonsense. Furthermore, our adoption agency had been accredited to mediate in inter-country adoptions by the American State Department in accordance with the Hague Convention. How much more reliable can an adoption agency be?

Our lawyers wiped the floor with the argument that Jeff had adopted the children in an attempt to circumvent the law. It is not fraud or deception if an US citizen follows the advice, legislation and guidelines of a US institution within the US. We had also completed the procedure up to and including the declaration that we were fit to adopt in Belgium. The court in Illinois declared that our family was a suitable environment for our children. We had never concealed any information whatsoever from anyone. Our opposing party could suggest this, but they could not prove it. We were two white men with two black daughters. How on earth could we look inconspicuous if we wanted to smuggle our children out of the country? The very idea!

I thought it was unforgivable that the DIA kept repeating this accusation. They had never contacted their American counterparts, who are responsible for drawing up regulations in the US, about Jeff's "deception". Unfortunately it is all too easy for civil servants to impose their interpretation of certain legislation upon powerless citizens. Apparently, having an adult conversation which might solve the problem with a foreign colleague of equal status might be a bit more daunting.

Our lawyers also hammered hard on the fact that the DIA was completely ignoring the best interests of the children. This was later to prove a huge weakness in their argument. I am still stunned by their attitude. The DIA, which is supposed to be the most effective guardian for adopted children brought to Belgium, was behaving as though considering and protecting the best interests of the children was not within their remit.

I also translated all this into English. It was an exhausting task and I sometimes felt as if it was draining me of every last ounce of energy.

4 October 2010
Today, Jeff started his new job in Paris. The plan was to live there with the children, but the move had to be postponed because of our problems in Belgium.

Nevertheless, we had gone ahead with house hunting, and had found a flat in the lively Île de la Cité, in the heart of the city just opposite Sainte-Chapelle. It is a dream location. The flat is full of character, style and charm and has the most wonderful view. We stayed there regularly with the girls, so that Ella and Maya would not have to miss Daddy too much during the working week. We took them to the little playground near Notre Dame, or the Luxembourg Gardens with its enormous lawns, or Centre Pompidou, where the colorful collection enchanted them. Sometimes we took a boat trip on the Seine to enjoy the constantly changing views and the water. Occasionally we took Jocelyne, our faithful babysitter, with us so that Jeff and I could have dinner in the city and spend some time together. Sometimes Jeff would give me the weekend off as a present. On Friday evening I would leave the children with Jeff in Brussels and spend the weekend visiting bookshops and museums, enjoying a delicious lunch or dinner, or just strolling in one of the charming neighborhoods of this wonderful city.

Poor Jeff – on top of all the stress we were enduring he was also having to adjust to a new job. He is a wonderful man, and my admiration for his professional drive and appetite for hard work is among the many reasons why I love him.

I continued to run our household in Brussels alongside my job in communication. It was becoming more difficult to combine everything, partly because I was spending so much time on the court case. I was so scared that we were going to lose it. All the uncertainty was making me feel powerless; like a plaything of hostile government officials. Sometimes I felt almost driven mad with despair. I had to keep busy to combat these feelings of powerlessness. Jeff has a calmer nature, but even he fell victim to these kinds of emotions sometimes.

18 October 2010

We finally received news from our contact person Jen, from Children's Issues in Washington DC.

On 1 October they had sent a letter to the Head of Department of the DIA in Brussels (whether this was anything to do with our prompting or not I don't know). Jen did not inform us as to the content of the letter, as it was correspondence between governments and not intended for outsiders. We just had to accept that for the time being.

It seemed that the case had finally escalated to a higher level. Jen named several managers at Children's Issues, as well as the Director, who were now all being kept informed of our case.

We were happy! Finally things were moving!

A day later we received a message from the American Embassy. As usual it was friendly and sympathetic, and reiterated the main points of the message from Children's Issues. They also asked us to keep them informed, and reassured us that people at the embassy were following the case closely.

This did us good.

We were due to go to court on the sixth of December in just seven weeks' time. Finally.

9 *November* 2010

Good news. The children's guardian called to say that the Office of Immigration Issues was going to issue a residence permit for one year. We could collect identity cards for our girls from the municipal authorities. They had actually contacted us, saying that they were pleased that they had finally been able to do something to help us. And, the girls had Jeff's family name on the cards.

The guardian also told us not to worry that the girls might be deported: their future was in Belgium, so much was clear. What a relief!

When I called Mr Deboutte to tell him our good news, he had another piece of good news for us. He had just received the ruling on a similar case, heard before the same judge in Brussels, forcing the Belgian State to recognize a foreign adoption. He warned us that the two cases were not the same, but it was still good news, as it indicated that this judge is at least prepared to be reasonable. Mr Deboutte was going to try to persuade the opposing party in the case (the DIA, which was also our opposing party) not to appeal against this decision in the interests of the adopted child and so that the family would no longer have to live with the uncertainty.

That evening I sat up in bed, reading through everything again on my laptop. Just for a while it looked as if everything was going to be fine.

30 November 2010

The presiding judge who had been appointed to hear our case was unable to make it on 6 December, the date set for the hearing.

On the phone, Ms Vandenberghe explained to us that it was not a bad sign that our case had been postponed. It could mean that the presiding judge was genuinely interested in hearing our case for herself.

However, it meant that the case would be postponed until the following year. If this was a film you would be rolling your eyes in disbelief by now at the cheap tricks being used to create extra tension and suspense.

2 December 2010

An e-mail arrived from Mr Deboutte entitled "appeal".

It said: "I would like to inform you that in the case of my [other] client the [DIA] has announced that it plans to appeal the judgment of the Court of First Instance in Brussels."

My stomach turned over. This meant that even if we won our court case, the DIA might well take it to an appeal. This meant another long wait not knowing what was going to happen. And then, after that...what?

But the news also gave me new insights.

These DIA officials did not care about finding a solution. They were not interested in the common good, or in serving the public. Society's interests are not served by tearing families apart and forcing them to live in a state of permanent insecurity about their status.

They are not even interested in complying with the law. If a citizen goes to court to have an adoption recognized and to overturn an official's decision, and the court then rules that the adoption must be recognized, this implies that the adoption is seen to be valid. I can imagine that any assertive official would want to present their point of view in court, but why would they then appeal if the decision went against them? Of course it costs a civil servant nothing to pursue the bee in their bonnet through the courts. All the extra lawyer's fees, court costs and time are paid for from the public purse, and I suppose when you're so intent on making a point it's easy to overlook the harm you're doing to individuals.

I tried to imagine why the officials at the DIA were behaving like this. Did they just want to demonstrate their power? To exert influence? To relieve their own frustration by taking it out on innocent people?

I also began to wonder whether the Minister of Justice was actually aware of the way his officials were operating. Surely he would not go along with this if he knew.

Slowly it began to dawn on us that if we won in the Court of First Instance, we would somehow have to find a way of making it impossible to appeal a decision in our favor. I had no idea how we would do this, but the alternative was a legal battle that could drag on for years, and that might be more than our family could bear.

31 December 2010

We were just back from a week in the US. Once again we had undertaken the ten hour flight followed by a two hour car journey to spend Christmas with our family.

The outbound flight was exhausting. Our wide-awake daughters were walking by now and wanted to show off their new skill every chance they got. They only slept for an hour. As usual, we could rely on first class treatment from the cabin crew, and our daughters charmed several complete strangers on the flight. They weren't bothersome or annoying, just very excited!

Christmas was peaceful. Mom and Dad were delighted to see their granddaughters and overwhelmed them with presents ("just another little something for the girls").

Jeff and I had resolved a few private matters. Because Jeff's new job was extremely demanding, I had offered to take a sabbatical, so that he wouldn't have to worry about the household for a while. We had enough worries without making life more difficult for ourselves by coping with the day to day practicalities of two careers. Jeff was relieved that I had suggested this myself: "It would be such a relief for me if you did, but I would never ask you. I know how important your job is to you." My work is important, but our family is even more important. I decided to bite the bullet and hand in my notice in January.

New Year's Eve was wonderful. We were invited to spend it with our friends Raïssa and Neil, together with Tom and Joep, and my sister Joke and her husband Ruben. All the children were there. It was a lovely, cozy evening with lots of laughter, great food (lobster) and champagne. Our daughters played until late in the evening. They are always at their best in a warm, sociable environment like this one (although I also suspected that their wakefulness may have had something to do with jet lag). At midnight, Jeff and I wished each other Happy New Year, and we both knew what we wanted more than anything else. Please let 2011 be the year that our legal nightmare ended so that we could enjoy being with our daughters without this endless anxiety.

14 January 2011
We still did not know what the DIA had said in reply to the official letter from its American colleagues.

After some prodding – we had got good at it by this point – we received a mail from Jen at Children's Issues. The tone was rather dry. It said: "We received an answer from the Belgian [DIA], but the only option they presented was the legal option that you are already pursuing in order to have your daughters' adoption recognized. [...] I am sorry that the [DIA's] answer was not more encouraging and I wish you the very best of luck with your case in the Belgian legal system."

7 | The Judge and the District Attorney

16 January 2011

I received an unexpected phone call from someone I didn't know. She introduced herself as an American mother with an adopted baby, who had recently moved to Belgium with her family because of her husband's job. She had been given our telephone number by our American social worker Bonnie.

She was very worried.

She and her husband had adopted their son in the US, at around the same time as they were moving to Belgium. She had registered her son in the Belgian municipality she lived in, and had shown them all the required adoption papers from the US. She had known she had to make sure the municipality was aware of the adoption, because she'd looked up all the formalities she would need to complete beforehand. So far, so good. So what was the problem?

A week ago, an attaché from the Inter-Country Adoption Service DIA (I later found out it was the same woman who was dealing with our case) phoned the woman at home. At first, the attaché made a fuss about her not speaking Dutch, but she switched to English once she realized she had no choice. She began to interrogate the woman about her son's adoption. What had they done? Who had given them permission to adopt the child? Who had they worked with in the US? Did the American government know? What had they said at city hall?

As she told me her story – obviously distressed – shivers ran down my spine. So these officials were phoning people at home to interrogate them about the most intimate details concerning their family.

"Bonnie told me to contact you, because you were also having problems". I confirmed that our "problem" was going to court next week. I didn't mention many of the details because I didn't want to make the poor woman even more worried than she already was. I advised her to make an appointment with a lawyer immediately, and gave her the contact details for ours. I told her not to lose hope, but also not to be naive.

I felt so sorry for her. It was impossible for me to share her hopes that the matter would be brought to a swift and successful conclusion.

Time would prove me right.

The attaché from the DIA contacted the municipality in which the family lived and forced the mayor and registrar to remove the child from the population register. The mayor was so embarrassed by this that he later visited the family to offer his personal apologies. The child's identity papers had to be handed back. This made him a "non-accompanied minor" in Belgian territory without a valid residence permit. The family applied to have the adoption recognized in Belgium, but the verdict arrived in just two weeks: request refused. The attaché from the DIA was kind enough to call the mother beforehand to inform her of the decision – so that she would "not be shocked" when she received the decision by post. She also told her that her adoption would *never* be recognized in Belgium. Soon after this the accumulated stress triggered a serious back problem, and this poor woman had to stay in bed for twelve weeks. A guardian was appointed for the child (the same one as ours, it's a small world). The family fled the country before their case could come to court, and the husband's employer transferred him to another European country where, fortunately, they had no problem getting their adoption recognized.

This family's fate made us even more convinced that we had been right to inform the embassy and Office of Children's Issues as soon as our problems started. Adoption should not be a stick that government officials can use to beat families with. It is a matter that must be solved by the countries involved. Agreements must be made on how domestic and other options in the US will be recognized in Belgium, without putting the families involved through so much trauma.

But neither the woman nor I knew all this that day. We met the family a few weekends later. Their son was a cute little blonde boy, about a year younger than our girls. He could already sit up.

24 January 2011
D-Day.

We dropped our daughters off at crèche, and went to the Palace of Justice, or rather the building beside it that houses the Court of the First Instance.

We were too early, so we took our places in the waiting room.

Jeff leafed nervously through the statement that he was going to read to the judge. I paced around and fiddled with my smartphone.

A middle-aged woman came up the stairs and took a seat beside a mousy young woman with long straight hair. They did not look at us. I knew without ever having seen them before that they were the attaché and the head of unit of the DIA. It was thanks to them that our adoption had not been recognized.

I had to sit down because I felt sick. How was it possible that they were here? They had never wanted to meet us. Two sentences in an e-mail seemed to be the most they could muster. These women knew absolutely everything about us: our relationship, our children, even the date we were married was all in our case file, which also contained dozens of photos of us and the children.

Why were they here? Did they want to put pressure on their lawyer, who had lost a similar case before the same judge just a few months ago? Were they particularly interested in our case because the American government had written to them about it? Were they trying to intimidate us?

As these thoughts flashed through my mind I felt the anger rise up in me. For the next two hours, I was going to have to use every ounce of self-control I possessed or I would explode.

Our lawyers arrived, and I told them that it looked as if our case apparently merited a bit of extra attention.

Ms Vandenberghe looked as if she was pleased by this. I saw a look of dogged determination on her face which I had not seen there before.

Finally, we were shown into the judge's chambers. The lawyer from the opposing party (the Ministry of Justice) was a friendly woman, who looked very young. The hearing began. The judge was a middle-aged woman with an open face. She was to remain friendly towards us throughout the hearing.

The hearing began. Before the lawyer from the opposing party could say the girls' birth names, the judge interrupted "Yes, yes, let's just call them *Ella and Maya*."

Our side was the first to speak. Both our lawyers stated our case. During her plea, Ms Vandenberghe dealt with the Justice Ministry's DIA arguments for refusing to recognize our adoption one by one, demolishing them with the sort of focused precision that you see in American courtroom dramas. I thought she was magnificent (and I told her so afterwards). Jeff and I were silent.

It was then the turn of the opposing party to state their case. The longer their lawyer talked, the more I got the feeling that she wasn't totally happy about representing this case. She looked like a soft-hearted woman, and I almost felt sorry for her. Her clients, the two officials, followed the proceedings with blank expressions. At one point, the youngest gave me an insolent stare, not averting her gaze when I chanced to look up, but continuing to stare at me. I looked away, embarrassed. What did she think she was playing at?

At one point, the opposing party said — for the third time — that "It may well be legally possible for LGBTs to adopt children in an inter-country adoption, but in practice, no such opportunity exists". To which – finally – our lawyer said: "Colleague, do you want us to go to the press immediately with your comments? My client's sexual orientation has nothing to do with his fitness to adopt or with whether or not this adoption can be recognized!"

The judge intervened: "Counsel Vandenberghe is right. I find your constant references to this man's sexual orientation irritating. This is a democratic country, governed by democratic laws that entitle gays and lesbians to adopt; therefore sexual orientation has no bearing on this case."

I felt the atmosphere in the room shift – to our advantage. The lawyer for the opposition was blushing.

When our lawyer finally asked the opposing party what solution they proposed she said: "It is not within the power of the DIA to find a solution for the children. It is the guardian's task to propose a solution. Maybe the children could remain in Belgium until they are eighteen as wards of the Belgian State [i.e. without any legally recognized parents in Belgium]."

To conclude, Ms Vandenberghe asked the judge whether Jeff was permitted to make a statement, and whether he could do so in English. The judge nodded.

Jeff looked down at his papers and started to read:

"Thank you, Your Honor. I am grateful that finally, after a year of waiting, someone wants to listen to us. I would like to elucidate a few points. First of all, you must realize that this is about my daughters ..."

All the bottled up emotions were too much for Jeff. He could not say anything and started to sob. I stood behind his chair and gently squeezed his shoulder.

You could have heard a pin drop in the Chamber. I saw that all three women from the opposing party were staring at the ground.

When Jeff was finally able to say "Sorry" to the judge, she spoke to him in English: "There is no need to say sorry. I understand how difficult this is for you. We have enough time and you must have your say."

Jeff was finally able to do so and I was so happy.

The opposing party's lawyer then said that, naturally, she was not suggesting that Jeff had not acted in the children's interests. To which our lawyer replied, "If that is your opinion, why are we here?"

The District Attorney who had followed the case from the sidelines, asked a few more questions. He seemed confused, and did not seem to be sure about the different roles of the Flemish adoption officer and the Inter-country Adoption Service of the federal Ministry of Justice. He looked good-natured, and in a different setting I would never have guessed that he represented the public role of District Attorney.

The judge brought the proceedings to a close and proposed that we reconvene within four weeks to discuss the recommendations of the District Attorney, which should have been completed by then.

We left the Chamber. The two DIA officials scuttled away as if the devil was snapping at their heels. Later I understood why. The three lawyers were shaking hands in a collegial manner, and the opposition lawyer also shook hands with us. I wanted to shout "How can you sleep at night with a job like this?!", but I was too overcome.

We spoke briefly with our lawyers on the courtroom steps. They were optimistic. "It is not in the bag, but it went as well as could have been hoped. The judge wasn't happy with the way they kept going on about your sexual orientation." That hadn't escaped me. "In a previous case, the procurator delivered a short, positive recommendation (to have the adoption recognized) and I would not expect anything different now, as the facts are almost identical." That sounded logical. I had thought the District Attorney looked rather nice, if a bit nerdy.

Our mood was lighter on the way home than it had been on the way there. I was even able to enjoy the January sun on my face.

2 *February* 2011

It was time to register our daughters for a school online. There are too few places for the number of children living in Brussels, so I wanted to get it done early. Although the system was very simple, I kept receiving error warnings each time I tried to register.

It turned out that, according to the information on their social security card, the girls could not be registered because they had only a provisional residence permit. I would have to go to the Reception Centre for Foreign Newcomers in Brussels in order to have the computer settings overruled by an integration official.

I sat waiting among a mixed bunch of newcomers to Brussels. Many of the women were wearing headscarves. The friendly official told me that many of the mothers came here because they could not write. She could not have been more helpful.

I received an e-mail from her a few weeks later to ask us how we were doing and to wish us the best of luck with our case. I was able to tell her that our daughters had been accepted by the school of our choice.

I always found these small acts of kindness and support very touching.

7 February 2011

We received an e-mail from the embassy: "We are keeping our fingers crossed here [at the embassy] hoping that your case will be resolved quickly. Your hearing was on 24 January, two weeks ago already. Has there been any progress?"

Jeff sent an extensive report to both the Embassy and Children's Issues in Washington. We asked if there was anything else that the Embassy thought it could do. We also asked if Children's Issues had heard anything from their Belgian colleagues at the DIA (after all they had taken the trouble to turn up at court, especially for us ...)

The answer from the Embassy didn't help much, but at least it was sympathetic: "... the Office of Children's Issues [in Washington] must take the lead in a case like this."

This sounded like a rather cautious confession: we would *like* to help you, but those people in Washington won't *allow* us to.

The reply from the Office of Children's Issues didn't arrive until two weeks later, after some prompting from us: "[...] I am sorry to inform you that there do not appear to be any options other than the legal proceedings you are currently engaged in. The Belgian DIA has made it clear to us that the legal proceedings are the only solution available to you [...]."

The embassy felt that the responsibility for an initiative lay firmly with Children's Issues, and Children's Issues accepted the explanation that the Belgian official had sent them by e-mail. *That was it?* Clearly our case wasn't sufficiently *high profile* to warrant more than this token effort – or so it seemed.

Meanwhile, the news in Belgium was dominated by the case of a little boy with a Belgian father (one half of a gay couple) and a surrogate mother in the Ukraine. The Belgian Department of Foreign Affairs had refused to issue a passport for the little boy, who had spent almost two years in an orphanage and with foster parents in the Ukraine. There was widespread public indignation when the two Belgian fathers went public with their story. How could bureaucracy and the wielders of red tape be permitted to let a child down so badly? Interestingly, shortly after this the men received a positive ruling from a Belgian court, and Foreign Affairs waived their right to appeal against it (maybe because they no longer dared to). The boy was finally able to come and live with his fathers. I cried buckets of tears as I watched the story of this family unfold on television.

Friends and family pointed out this case to us, saying: "You should go to the press. That would stop those terrible officials in their tracks."

We were a bit dubious about this, and our lawyers were also not in favor. They pointed out that there was no guarantee that this tactic would work and that our privacy might be a very high price to pay for little return.

The American Embassy also let us know that they were following the case of the surrogate mother, without suggesting what they thought was so inspiring about it. Did they want us to go to the press? Would they be willing to support us if we did?

24 February 2011

To our lawyers' amazement and our dismay, the District Attorney advised the judge not to recognize the adoption in his written recommendation.

He stated the rules that had been violated, adding that we could "still regularize this [in a different way]". He neglected, however, to say *how* this could be done.

At the hearing four days later, our lawyers asked the District Attorney to explain how we could "regularize" the situation. They referred to the opposing party, who still clung to their position that the one and only way to regularize this situation was through this court. They also referred to the fact that the Flemish adoption officer had told us that she could do nothing more for us.

As I had expected, the District Attorney was not able to explain his recommendation properly. It was clear to me that he was not really familiar with the subject matter. When our lawyers confronted him with the fact that in a similar case a few months ago he had advised the court to *recognize* the adoption, he seemed unable to remember it. (Or was he just pretending?) Our lawyers kept on pointing out the inconsistencies, and asked the judge to disregard his recommendations. The District Attorney kept leafing through the recommendation, trying to find relevant passages with which to reply to all this, but he could not find anything. I began to wonder if he had even written the recommendation himself.

It is outrageous that someone is allowed to voice an opinion on such important issues who either knows nothing about them, or is simply not interested.

The judge said that she would consider the matter and issue a ruling within thirty days (in the end it was to be ninety).

Our lawyers seemed quite positive, but I was not convinced that the District Attorney and his point of view had been effectively neutralized.

8 | The Ambassador

28 February 2011

We had been approached several times during the past few months by American citizens living in Belgium, asking us how they should go about adopting a child from the US.

Jeff wrote another long e-mail to the embassy. The bottom line was that we may be the first to encounter problems with an American adoption in Belgium, but we will certainly not be the last.

We thought it was untenable for both the Embassy in Brussels and Children's Issues in Washington DC to persist in saying that they could do nothing. We asked for a meeting with the ambassador. We had waited long enough.

3 March 2011

A big and very welcome surprise. We received an e-mail from the American ambassador himself.

"Dear......,

I have followed your case with great interest and concern. I have now received permission from Washington to become actively involved in your case. In order to draw up a good plan of action, I would like to be fully briefed by you and your lawyer [...]."

We jumped for joy.

Finally!

A meeting had already been planned for next Wednesday.

Jeff and I prepared an information folder, with a timeline of the events and a list of each of the Belgian and Flemish officials involved and their relevant minister; all of them people who could *potentially* play a positive role in our case. We went without our lawyers ("By now you know your case better than I do, said Ms Vandenberghe).

At the embassy, we first had to go through a security check. The ambassador's assistant, a friendly, middle-aged American woman, was waiting for us. In the lift she told us that everyone at the embassy was very concerned about us and that she was glad that we were finally able to visit. She asked to see a photo of our daughters (of course). We were led into a kind of comfortable bunker, which turned out to be the ambassador's office. There was a whole group of people around the table and they all introduced themselves as members of staff. I couldn't remember a single name. The ambassador, a slim, lively man, stood up from behind his desk and shook our hands warmly. "Welcome. I have been following your case from the beginning. When your mail arrived last week, I also decided that enough is enough. I now have permission to develop initiatives myself, naturally in collaboration with Washington."

So, it *had* been a turf war after all.

The ambassador asked us to retell our story in brief.

Jeff wanted to begin, but his breath caught and he had tears in his eyes. "Sorry," he said, "this is so hard on us."

I noticed that a woman on the other side of the table was also wiping away a tear (I later found out she was the Special Assistant to the Ambassador).

The ambassador listened to our story, asked a few questions and said "This is just outrageous."

I couldn't have put it better myself.

Someone asked if we had considered moving to the US. Jeff

said: "Only the children and I have American passports."

I said: "I'm not going to flee my country like a thief in the night."

The ambassador said that we could count on him. He had already planned to bring up the subject next week with the Flemish Minister-President, whom he referred to as 'a good friend'. "I have accrued a good deal of political capital since I arrived here, and now I'm going to spend it."

He sounded completely sincere. I suggested that he could also target the Federal Minister of Justice, as after all he was the boss of the DIA.

He did not react to my suggestion. Much later, I found out that the ambassador had not expected much from the Minister of Justice. I heard from various sources that this Minister simply does not respond to many phone calls from the embassy; not in this case or any other.

We once more emphasized the fact that we may be the first case that the embassy knows about, but we will not be the last. Sure enough, a week later the American family, who we knew quite well by now, was also received at the embassy with their son.

An hour later we were outside again. We could hardly believe it. Finally somebody decent and straightforward had said that he was willing to see this through with us. We had an ally!

Communication with Children's Issues was a lot less straightforward. Jeff and I had decided not to stop nagging them to keep looking for a solution. It was still totally unclear what they were actually thinking and doing. They continued to ignore our request to see the correspondence between them and the Belgian DIA.

Children's Issues let us know that they were "working on promoting an adoption channel between Flanders and the US" without explaining how this could be of any use to us. Anyway, we had encountered the Flemish adoption officer and were only too well aware of her attitude towards US adoptions. We were pretty sure that she would not cooperate with any efforts to bring this about.

Children's Issues also said something that we refused to let pass unchallenged: "the US adoption service, in your case and other cases, has acted on the basis of their understanding of US legislation and policy, which considers citizens of the US as resident in US territory even if they live abroad. Since your case has been brought to our attention, we have changed our guidelines [...]. We have informed the Belgian DIA of our amended guidelines and hope that a solution can be found in your case as well as for other cases in the interests of the children."

Jeff blew up. Not only was this incorrect but making this statement to the Belgian DIA could harm our case; and feel like an admission of wrongdoing. To us it felt as if Children's Issues were trying to rewrite history, not to mention blaming somebody else for their own mistake. An error on the part of the US authorities is not the same as US adoption agencies and citizens misinterpreting the guidelines published by Children's Issues. We got the impression that Children's Issues was trying to suggest that adoption agencies and courts in the US had exceeded their remit, even though they had acted in accordance with clear guidelines from their own government.

We were sick and tired of Children's Issues and their ambivalent attitude. We had been patient for long enough. The time had come for them to take a stance.

We sent a long letter in reply, and we did not mince our words.

The tone was either going to have the desired effect or turn them against us completely, but it was what it was – a cry of desperation.

11 April 2011

We received a long e-mail from the Office of Children's Issues, this time from the boss of our contact person Jen.

It had a sympathetic tone – and something that was new. It was open. It replied to all the points that we had made earlier.

"[…] We know how difficult this process has been for you and your family. We hope that the impending ruling in Brussels will turn matters in a positive direction. […] We have discussed what we can do to help you with the Embassy in Brussels […]."

When talking about finding an alternative solution to a legal battle, it said:

"We have told the Belgians that we are prepared to effect a retroactive Hague adoption in the case of your daughters if that would be an option [for the Belgians]. […] We are sympathetic to the fact that you and your adoption agency acted in accordance with US legislation and regulations [concerning domestic adoptions]. Unfortunately at the time of your adoption process our guidelines did not place sufficient emphasis on the fact that the regulations of the country in which the US citizen is currently residing may apply and that these regulations may have a different interpretation of the term 'residency'. […]

About the correspondence with the Belgians:

"We consider that by informing the Belgians that our guidelines have been updated we have transferred responsibility for the implementation of a domestic adoption from you and your adoption agency to us as the Central Authority. It also underlines our commitment to cooperating [with the Belgians] in the interests of the children."

They also added all the correspondence between them and the Belgians, both e-mails and official letters.

I was relieved. At last it looked as if Washington had finally woken up.

17 April 2011

We read the correspondence between the Belgians and the Americans with interest.

A few things were crystal clear.

Despite the fact that we had first made contact with Children's Issues back in March 2010, the case was only being followed up now (at our insistence).

But much worse was the content and tone of the answers from the Belgians. The tone was arrogant and rude. This could only have been the work of the two women we had seen in the courtroom. Their replies contained a few well-aimed blows below the belt directed at the Americans.

First of all, the Belgian DIA was acting as if the Hague Convention between Belgium and the USA did not exist. They subjected every aspect of the US adoption policy to minute scrutiny, as if it were highly suspect, but never pointed out a single element in our American procedure that had failed to meet Belgian standards. I though the correspondence showed an appalling lack of respect for a Convention partner.

The DIA had also written that they had "questions regarding

the permissibility of LGBT adoptions in the US." Once more, I was shocked that they had the nerve to put that in black and white, thereby insinuating that Jeff had lied about his sexual orientation. The DIA had nothing to do with the assessment of an adoptive parent's sexual orientation in any country! Furthermore, our orientation had nothing whatsoever to do with whether or not the adoption was legal. Or were they trying to say that this was not the case in supposedly progressive Belgium?

The Belgian DIA stated that it was not for them to find a solution for our case. It was up to the public guardian to find a long-term solution which was in the children's interests. (How curious then, that they had not mentioned the public guardian once in their oral arguments during the court hearing. Could that have been because she was on our side and wished to see the adoption recognized?)

The wording of the letter, as well as the persistent but never substantiated allegations regarding 'the role of money' in US adoptions, made it clear that the DIA considered adoptions in the US to be morally inferior.

Finally came the epitome of diplomatic rudeness: the DIA did not even address its replies to the person who had written to them, but to a random attaché whose e-mail address they happened to have – our contact person, Jen.

Why had Children's Issues not written a stinging reply to the Belgians? Were they also stunned?

1 May 2011
We decided to go to the US for a spring break. We would visit friends in Washington and then have a week at the seaside in

Delaware.

It would take our minds off waiting for the ruling on our case.

The decision was due any day, but we figured it was more fun biting your nails on holiday than at home.

We had also been invited to a meeting in Washington DC with the Office of Children's Issues. Well actually we'd invited ourselves, but to our surprise they'd immediately replied that we would be welcome!

We received an email from the American ambassador, who knew we were going to the US. He said that we should know that "the ball is now actually in our [the Embassy in Brussels] court. [...] We do not know how successful we will be, but we are now actively involved. [...]. As always, we will keep you informed."

In other words; by all means go to a meeting in Washington DC, but from now on Children's Issues would know that it was the Embassy in Brussels that was calling the shots!

9 May 2011

Today we were going to downtown Washington DC for our meeting at the Office of Children's Issues.

Our friend Michael had offered to look after the girls during the meeting. It was a beautiful spring day, the city was green and full of life and light.

We first found the building, and then went for a sandwich nearby. I had to force myself to eat, as my throat felt as if it had been clamped shut.

Just before one, we made our way into the large office building with glass doors. We were well prepared, and I had resolved not to get angry as that would only distract me from the matter at hand.

When we got out of the lift there was a woman waiting to show us to the room where the meeting would take place. The room contained an enormous oval wooden table, black leather chairs and the walls were paneled in cherry wood. *Very boardroom.*

Then I noticed that places had been reserved for us. On the right hand side of the table were two white name boards with our names printed in black ink. On the other side of the table there were eight name cards, extending along almost the entire length of the table. Jeff also noticed this, and said "Wow! They got out the big guns for this." I hissed between my teeth: "This is the oldest trick in the book. Now they are going to intimidate us because they are in the majority. Do they really think we are going to fall for that one?" Strangely enough, I was not paralyzed by the stress. On the contrary, I felt extremely clear-headed.

The director of the Office of Children's Issues was seated opposite Jeff. Up until now, we'd had hardly any contact with him. Beside him, and opposite me, was the place reserved for the woman who was 'Special Advisor to the Secretary of State [Hillary Clinton] for Children's Issues'.

Good, I thought. They finally get it.

People drifted into the room and introduced themselves to us. They were all very friendly. I immediately recognized the woman who had to be the Special Advisor to Hillary Clinton. She was well coiffed, and was wearing chic clothes and serious jewelry.

Everyone sat down and the director welcomed us. The Special Advisor then pointed to my watch (my most recent Valentine's present from Jeff): "Lieven, is that the real thing?" "Of course", I said. "Do I look like someone who wears fake jewelry?" We immediately bonded.

Jeff started the meeting: "We have brought documents for you containing the most important events in our case. First of all, I would like to thank you for meeting us, because this is really.......... ..." He fell silent and bowed his head.

I touched his leg under the table and took over from him.

I did not beat around the bush. We said everything we had to say — the people on the other side of the table listened and interrupted us just occasionally to ask a question. The Director listened without saying anything.

First of all I went over the timeline of events, naming the contact persons within the Belgian and Flemish governments. Jeff and I then gave an overview of the solutions that were still possible. And then we had a few things we needed to get off our chest.

We said that we were deeply disappointed that the Office had just changed the information on their website without first reaching a compromise or long-term solution with the Belgians.

We were also sorry that our case had not been immediately handled with the urgency that it required.

The reply that the Belgians had written to the letter from Children's Issues was full of accusations against the American authorities and adoption services, accusations that had never been refuted. I asked the Director whether it was possible he might agree with the Belgian allegations (By this time, I was getting angry. Afterwards, Jeff said to me dryly: "Lieven, it is never a good idea to use the word 'fuck' when you are talking to representatives of the American government").

We warned that the US should not cherish any illusions: if we won our case in the Court of First Instance, the Belgians would take us to the court of Appeal. The American excuse that they could not intervene in an ongoing court case did simply not hold water. This case could drag on for another ten years. What were the Americans planning to do? Spend the next ten years following all this from the sidelines?

Finally, we said that we had requested a meeting with Children's Issues because we felt that there had been a lack of clarity, and that scant interest had been taken in our situation. We hoped that this was no longer the case.

The Director came to a decision, saying "Your story is very clear. You came here to ask us for help and I can assure you that you will get it."

A weight fell from my shoulders. The American Embassy had got our message and now so had Children's Issues. There was nothing more we could do.

We left for Delaware, for another week at Rehoboth Beach.

11 *May* 2011

The Embassy in Brussels was true to its word. We received a mail saying that there had been a meeting between the American Ambassador and the Flemish Minister-President. The new deputy head of cabinet of the Ministry of Welfare was also present. This woman had asked the people from the embassy if it would be possible to meet us.

As we were in the US, we suggested holding a telephone conference, as we didn't want to wait.

The conversation took place at 8.30 in the morning US time. We had already been awake for a few hours (children + jet lag). Jeff spoke to the woman first and then I took it from there.

I thanked her expressly, because it was the first time in a year that someone from the cabinet had even acknowledged our existence.

I told our story for the thousandth time. Naturally I got bogged down in details here and there and had some difficulty controlling my emotions, but she listened to it all politely and asked if I could send some additional information. Of course I could! I did that immediately from my laptop, wondering what on earth this charming woman must have thought of me after this first, ranting, conversation.

It was simple. Everything had just become too much, both for Jeff and for me. The stress of the meeting two days ago combined with a lack of sleep, all the worry and the enervating wait for the judge's decision, which should have come ages ago, had been taking its toll.

13 *May* 2011

The American Ambassador in Brussels had personally written the longest e-mail we had so far received. He must have had his colleagues in Washington on the line.

The mail expressed a lot of understanding for us. The tone seemed to be: OK, you guys really had your say over there, but now you have to listen carefully to me.

"Thank you for your e-mail. We understand all too well the stress that this situation has caused you.

[...]

I understand that for you, as a parent, the coordination process between governments must have been, and continues to be, frustrating. However, I can assure you that the people handling this case in Washington have done so with care, a sense of duty and professionalism. Naturally, it would be best if the people at Children's Issues in Washington could come to a long-term solution with [the Belgians]. Normally, that would be the only manner in which to solve a policy dispute such as this. That is why [...] progress may appear to be slow and unsatisfactory despite the good intentions, professionalism and sense of duty of the people involved.

[...] The changes to the website [containing information from Children's Issues], [...] were not made with the intention of harming your case. These changes were necessary in order to prevent other people finding themselves in a situation similar to your own.

[...] I am cautiously optimistic that we can reach a swift solution.

[...] With regard to your concern that "Washington just gave in to the Belgians and is more concerned about its international relations than protecting its own citizens", I think that the tone from Washington was correct and necessary.

[We] cannot achieve much by banging our fists on the table.

We have been able to confirm our credibility (our integrity, transparency and mutual respect) and friendship with the Belgian authorities [in the short period that I have been ambassador here]. This friendship has made it possible for us to discuss your case almost immediately at the highest [Belgian] level. The same friendship and credibility have enabled me to express quite clearly how disappointing the Belgian treatment of our citizens has been in this case. We did not hold back because there was no need to. [...] We have accrued a considerable capital [of goodwill, in Belgium] and we have been able to spend it on this important case."

I was so grateful to this man. He, the most visible American ambassador to Belgium ever, was so much more than a public figurehead. He had gone to so much trouble for us. He was very clear. He promised to do his best for us but made no guarantees. He was a man after my own heart.

It was only at this point that I was able to relax and enjoy our holiday a little. I still checked our e-mails every day to see whether our lawyer had received a court decision, but apart from that we had a peaceful, harmonious trip.

We had invited Jeff's parents to stay at the same hotel in Rehoboth (a late Christmas present). It was lovely to see our daughters playing, singing and laughing with their grandparents. Every so often the weather was even good enough to go to the beach (our daughters still liked to eat sand).

1 June 2011

Jeff and I decided that we were no longer going to wait passively to see what other people could do for us. We had realized a few things during the past few weeks.

First, our best chance of a quick solution was to win our court case. A decision in our favor would be an enormous step towards reaching our goal. If the opposing party decided to appeal, we would have a short period in which to lobby our case to influential politicians or interest groups, or to somehow find a way to prevent an appeal.

Secondly, *we* were in the best position to lobby for our own case. I was now looking after the children full-time. The girls went to crèche three times a week, so I could use this free time for our own lobbying activities.

While waiting for the court decision (and hoping it was in our favor) I made a list of interest groups and politicians who might be interested on our case.

I sent another mail to the Flemish Minister of Equal Opportunities. Despite a great deal of e-mail correspondence with his advisor I had never been able to find out what the department could do for us or whether they had already done anything. I addressed my e-mail directly to the minister.

The answer came almost immediately. The minister's assistant was going to pick a date in the very near future. Hurray!

I also requested a meeting with Çavaria, the gay rights group.

8 June 2011
Today I had my meeting with the Flemish Minister for Equal Opportunities.

I took an information folder, so that he could read through everything if he wanted.

I was immediately shown into a large office with wooden walls and a beautiful view of Brussels. The minister himself was there with his advisor.

The minister listened briefly and said: "We can do something. Adoption is already difficult enough without having to go through all this as well." I gave a small internal sigh of relief.

The minister agreed to undertake the following actions: he would phone the Minister of Justice that very day and discuss our case at the level of the Flemish government with his colleague from Welfare. He promised to phone me back with the first feedback.

Within half an hour I was back out on the street. Unbelievable. Why had we waited so long to do this, thinking that other people would do it for us?

The minister did call me back. He had spoken to the Minister of Justice and the State Secretary for Family Policy. In the corridors of the Flemish parliament he had also spoken to his Flemish colleague for Welfare, who had said that there would be a meeting in two days' time with the officials from Justice involved in our case. The Flemish standpoint would be that Flanders wanted to change its attitude to American adoptions and that it was in this spirit that they would ask their federal colleagues to find a solution for our case — or if we won our case, not to launch an appeal.

The mail that we received from Çavaria was in sharp contrast to the minister's forthright approach: "Could you specify what you expect from us, or what your specific questions are? [...] It is usually very difficult to intervene in personal cases."

It was enough to make you explode!

13 June 2011

A mail from the Director of Children's Issues! For the first time since we started our correspondence with them we have received concrete information about the actions being undertaken.

"My departments have prepared a letter for the Belgian Minister of Justice containing an answer to Belgium's concerns with regard to US adoptions. We have also attached guidelines on how we could re-process your adoption (...) if the Flemish adoption officer is prepared to cooperate with us on that point."

Wow! People were finally reaching out a helping hand instead of slamming doors in our faces.

The Director asked us to keep them informed on how our court case was progressing.

Indeed, it was high time for us to finally hear the ruling of the court.

9 | "Leave our family in peace"

20 June 2011

Our lawyers had received the court's decision.

We had won.

To cut a long story short, the Flemish adoption officer had been heavily criticized for not doing enough to support us, and other couples, with the adoption process. The federal DIA was reprimanded for apparently assuming that "every adoption is, by definition, not in the child's interests", for having an overly formalistic approach and for totally ignoring the interests of the children involved.

I felt a little bit relieved, but I was still worried. If our opposition lodged an appeal all this might well have been for nothing.

My reaction surprised me. I had waited so long for this day, but now it had finally come I wasn't able to enjoy it.

We immediately relayed the decision to Washington, the Embassy, the Flemish Minister of Welfare and the Flemish Minister of Equal Opportunities. The next day there was a stream of e-mails back and forth to the American Embassy. The ambassador, who had been tirelessly and selflessly making efforts on our behalf, was on a trade mission with a number of top Belgian politicians. We understood that he would urge his Belgian partners to talk to the Minister of Justice about our case to persuade him not to initiate an appeal.

Our lawyers advised us not to serve notice of the judgment to the opposing party for as long as people were still lobbying for us, as this would initiate the start of the appeal period. Despite my impatience, I was willing to listen to their good advice. It would be better not to provoke the opposition at this point.

21 June 2011

We received a letter from the Flemish Minister of Welfare. His message was short and to the point: he had been informed of the court decision in our case and would urge his federal colleagues from Justice not to appeal this decision *in the interests of the children.*

An idea slowly took shape in my mind. What if we could bombard the person who had final responsibility for all this – the Minister of Justice – with letters from all the prominent people and organizations we could get on our side? They would all make the same request to the minister: "Please rein in your civil servants. Do not allow them to appeal. Leave this family in peace."

Jeff thought it was a brilliant idea.

In the days that followed, I finally had a meeting with Çavaria (I had told them that I had been given a meeting with the Minister of Equal Opportunities).

I also contacted *Regenbooghuis (The Rainbow House – a gay meeting center)*, the Belgian business association (a sort of club for gay professionals), the Brussels State Secretary for Equal Opportunities and a number of politicians who had been recommended to me, from every political quarter except Vlaams Belang (the extreme right party). In the weeks to come, I would be amazed at how easy it was to get support. Almost everyone I wrote to did something to help us. The members of parliament wrote to the Minister of Justice, or passed on the material to their party's specialist, who then contacted me.

The tone was always the same: we cannot believe that there are government officials who will not stop harassing you even after you have won your court case.

We also decided to write a letter to the Minister of Justice ourselves, because we had heard indirectly that the Minister had already been advised by his civil servants to lodge an appeal, otherwise we would think that we had set a precedent.

So we wrote it, in Jeff's name. It was the most passionate letter that we would ever write.

"[...] I therefore beg you to leave my family, and especially my children, in peace. Please let them keep their name and their parents.

I would also like to take this opportunity to point out to you that, even within your own administration, not everyone shares the DIA's opinion. Our children's guardian, who was appointed by your Public Guardian's Office [another service in your department], has submitted a written statement to the Court in Brussels saying that she wishes the adoption to be recognized because the children belong in our family.

Together with my embassy and the American FCA (the Office of Children's Issues, and their head Ms Hillary Clinton), I believe that the heart of the problem lies in a different interpretation of the Hague Convention and other legislation: what the US considers as a domestic adoption is seen here in Brussels as an inter-country adoption. [...]

It is beyond dispute that both countries share the same philosophy regarding adoption, in that it is a valuable alternative for children in need for whom no other suitable options are available. Both countries have implemented the principles of the Hague Convention on Adoption. [...]"

We received a few appreciative e-mails from the American officials in Brussels and Washington, who applauded the style of the letter: "a beautifully written letter", "from the heart".

22 June 2011

We had organized a birthday party for our daughters' second birthday. Family and friends, both with and without children, were invited. Jeff had made waffles and I'd baked pancakes and we had ordered a gigantic birthday cake from the baker.

It was a great party. The children kept running in and out, playing on the slide and chasing balls. Our daughters beamed all day and had fun until they literally dropped. I thought once more what a gift it was to be a father. I hoped with all my heart that this would be the last birthday that we would have such terrible worries about those dearest to us.

11 July 2011

My aunt Magda, who is politically active in Brussels, had taken me along with her to the City Hall for the annual reception in honor of The Day of the Flemish Community in Belgium.

Magda said that all the ministers and politicians who had any involvement, big or small, in our case would be there. She had also arranged for me to have dinner with a senator the week before. I had not known what to expect, but it had been a pleasant surprise. The senator turned out to be a woman doctor; sharp, witty and socially committed, who thought that it was only natural that she should write to the Minister of Justice on our behalf and ask him to leave our family in peace. Instead of a rushed bite to eat with a politician, I spent a wonderful evening in the company of a woman with an acute intellect and a big heart. The senator also promised to speak to a Flemish colleague from her party; one of the authors of the new Flemish decree on adoption.

My goal for this day, however, was to speak to the federal Minister of Justice, De Clerck, and the Flemish Minister of Welfare, Vandeurzen. I didn't know if this would be possible, but I was not going to let myself be discouraged easily.

In City Hall, the large reception room was full to bursting. Magda introduced me to a few people, including the current president of the Senate, Danny Pieters, who used to be an old professor of mine in Leuven. We recognized each other, and after a brief but warm exchange in which I explained our case once more — albeit in bullet points — he identified one of my targets for me: "There's your Minister, under that statue by the wall."

I made my way through the crowd towards the Minister of Justice, who was engaged in an animated conversation. I hovered around until the conversation ended and approached him.

The Minister automatically held out his hand. I said: "Hello sir. I have come here to see you. I don't know whether you know me. I have never begged anyone for anything in my life before, but I am doing so today: I implore you to please leave my family in peace." To my surprise, he got straight to the point of the matter. He said that he "still needed time". He had to "argue" our case, because failure to lodge an appeal could create a "precedent" that other couples would be able to follow; namely adopting children outside the framework of the authorized Flemish Community. "My civil servants only apply the law."

I could not agree with this last statement: "Sir, with all due respect, what your civil servants want to do to us has nothing to do with applying the law. I cannot imagine that any official with a shred of moral integrity can fail to realize that further action against us will destroy our family. You and your civil servants have discretionary powers. A judge has already pronounced a ruling against the decision taken by your civil servants. Why is that not sufficient? What you say is true: the basis of our problems lies with the Flemish adoption officer. But it is now your department that holds the key to the solution."

By then, the minister had had quite enough. He said: "Don't try to push me. We shall see. I will be in contact. Or rather, you will hear of our decision."

And off he went.

It took a while before the adrenaline level in my blood returned to normal.

OK. Now it was the turn of Vandeurzen, the Flemish Minister. I planned to make him aware that his federal colleague (and fellow party member) was shifting the blame for our problems onto him.

I found minister Vandeurzen a little later, managed to get him away from the group he was talking to and introduced myself to him. I told him that we had received a letter in which he had promised us that he would urge his federal colleague, Minister De Clerck, to leave us alone. I said that De Clerck had just told me that the cause of all our misery was the Flemish policy on adoption. The Minister looked a bit shocked (perhaps at my nerve?). He said: "I will have another word with him." I replied: "Sir, just talking won't help. I know that this is neither the time nor the place to have this debate, but unfortunately your Flemish adoption officer lacks moral integrity. And I think that you know this. I am therefore asking you personally to do something about it."

It was clear that his Excellency had also now heard more than enough. He waved his hand and said: "I will have another word with Stefaan."

Later that month we found out (via a source in the Flemish government) what else was going on. The federal Minister of Justice (of a federal state in political crisis) was in the process of resigning, and knew that there might be no place for him in the next government because his party had lost too many seats. This meant that he was in no mood to make decisions about controversial dossiers, not even at the request of members of his own party in the Flemish government. So that's why he wanted more time! More time, in this case, meant "Whoever takes over from me can sort this one out!"

But I had done what I came to do.

I had to get away from this crowded gathering. I said a quick goodbye to Aunt Magda and went to the *Grand Place* to catch my breath. The sun was shining but I felt exhausted.

14 July 2011

We received a message from the Centre for Equal Opportunities and Opposition to Racism, now known as the Interfederal Centre for Equal Opportunities and the Federal Centre of Migration. They were studying our "legally complex" dossier and requested a lot of additional information, which I sent them immediately. They later informed me that they had written a letter to the Flemish government and the authors of the new Flemish Adoption decree, to express their "deep concern" about the lack of compliance with the existing adoption legislation, in particular the section giving LGBT couples the same right to adopt as heterosexual couples. But they said it was "impossible" to lobby for us specifically to the ministers in question. By now, I was beginning to recognize that song. Once more I was left wondering what the point of an anti-discrimination center was if it was so reluctant to act on behalf of individuals, even though they thought that our case was important enough to merit a letter to the legislators involved.

2 August 2011

Today, after one and a half years of badgering, I finally had my meeting with Çavaria. I braced myself because I hadn't formed a very high opinion of this organization, but the conversation with their representative was cordial.

All of a sudden she said: "I hadn't realized your situation was as bad as this. We will definitely do something for you. We will write to both Ministers Vandeurzen and De Clerck. We would also be happy to support you if you decide to take your story to the press."

In the days and weeks that followed, she kept her word.

Jeff also received an e-mail from Priscilla*, an American lobbyist in Brussels who we were friendly with. Priscilla had an extensive network. We were at a brunch at her house one day when our story came up in conversation. She was shocked by it, as were all the other American guests at the table. Priscilla sent us an e-mail the next day, with a list of options and suggestions for press contacts and international journalists to whom she had already spoken. "With all the depressing economic news from the EU, I know you could count on a lot of interest from the journalists. They all want to report on something else occasionally, and your story is so moving. But everyone I knew said that we should wait until September. That was when everyone would be back from their holidays and the people who watch TV and read newspapers would be paying more attention.

A few days later, I received an unexpected message from the Interfederal Centre for Equal Opportunities and the Federal Centre of Migration, saying: "I wanted to let you know that I have written to the people responsible for submitting the proposal for the decree concerning the regulation of the inter-country adoption of children. I have submitted a few considerations and asked them to ensure that the rights of same-sex couples are respected. Restricting the intake [of prospective adoption parents] must not lead to the *de facto* exclusion of LGBTs, and a proactive study must be conducted into adoption channels which are open to same-sex couples.

Two of the people contributing to the proposal have already informed me that they are willing to discuss this in more detail [...]"

This was good news, even if it meant nothing for our case in concrete terms.

A day later Jeff could no longer contain himself, and he wrote a new letter to Minister Vandeurzen, saying that the Flemish and Federal authorities must stop trying to shift the blame onto each other. We asked the Minister of Welfare to cooperate instead with his federal colleague so that a long-term solution could finally be found for us. The simplest solution would be for the federal authorities to leave us in peace and not to appeal the court decision.

11 August 2011
Today I advanced my lobbying skills (which were pretty good by now) a stage further. I planned to begin an organized offensive,

and approach as many members of parliament as possible who might be sympathetic to our cause.

I was to be amazed by the amount of help and goodwill we found we could rely on. I had never met any of these people, but I was listened to by individual members of parliament, both Flemish and federal, from the VLD, N-VA, SP.A, and Groen! [Liberal Democrats, New Flemish Alliance, A Different Socialist Party and the Green Party]. Without hesitation they all promised to raise questions about our case to help resolve it. Some wrote warmly worded replies and expressed clearly what they thought of the way we had been treated. Letters of support like that really did us good.

18 August 2011

We received an important e-mail from Washington DC. In an attachment, it included the most recent letter that the Office of Children's Issues had sent to their counterparts in Belgium who were obstructing our adoption.

The letter contained a detailed reply to the Belgian objections to American adoptions as earlier expressed and raised during the court hearings.

The Americans expressed their satisfaction with the recent court ruling (their letter demonstrated their assumption that the case was closed).

They also wanted to prevent more Americans encountering such problems in Belgium, and to this end they officially refuted a number of Belgian "concerns".

They rejected the argument that USA failed to take into account the subsidiarity principle in inter-country adoptions. The

American interpretation of this principle rests upon existing doctrine in the Convention: The State of Origin will first consider possible options to place the child in its own country before deciding that an inter-country adoption is in the interests of the child. The Americans therefore did not agree with the Belgian interpretation that inter-country adoption should only be possible if *all* possibilities to place the child in its own country had been *exhausted*. The Americans considered the interests of the child first and foremost.

The Americans also refuted the Belgian accusation that birth parents in the US were able to decide who was allowed to adopt their child: the opinion of the birth parents may be one of the factors that a court takes into consideration, but it is never the only or deciding factor.

The US then dealt with the DIA's anti-gay argument. This argument insinuated that Jeff had somehow concealed his sexuality from the American court, as the DIA officials in Belgium doubted whether homosexuals were allowed to adopt in the US. The American answer to this was simple: they gave the Belgians a list of US states, via a web link, where LGBTs can adopt (naturally, Illinois is one). That was how easy it was to find out.

The Americans then provided a detailed rebuttal of the accusation that it is possible to "buy" children in the US (the much repeated allusions by the Belgians to the role of money in US adoptions). The Americans gave a list of American federal laws and Treaties that prohibit this. They also gave an overview of the cost-related factors involved in the adoption process.

In conclusion, the Americans expressed their hope that work could finally start on building an adoption channel between the US and Belgium.

I was so impressed that I re-read this letter several times.

One thing was now clear: if an appeal was launched after this letter it would cause a diplomatic incident. The Ministry of Justice could not just ignore this letter without paying a diplomatic price. For the first time since all this had started I felt a wave of energy rolling in our favor.

That was not all. There was a letter in the post from the Ministry of Justice's Public Guardian's Office. My hands were shaking as I opened it, and then I read the following:

"In view of the Court Ruling acknowledging the foreign adoption [...] the Public Guardian's Office hereby declares that their guardianship has ended by operation of law."

I could not believe it. I just could not believe it.

Surely the officials at the Public Guardian's Office knew that it would still be possible to appeal against the ruling? And that we could lose that appeal? Why were they doing this?

I could not help myself. I called the number on the letter and got a man on the other end of the line. It was the same sympathetic young man we had met more than a year ago.

First of all, I thanked him for his decision. Then I plucked up the courage to ask him if he was aware that a lot of things could still happen with regard to our case. His answer was clear:

"Sir, we used our discretionary powers in your case. We do not consider that there is any reason to continue the guardianship. Our guardians are there to help children who are in genuine need, not to play at politics. To be honest with you sir, we wish you the very best, and in all politeness, I hope that I never have to hear from you again."

He was short and to the point but this was great news!

In the days that followed we received a few e-mails from the

Flemish or federal members of parliament we had contacted, telling us that they would write to the two Ministers involved in our case because they wanted to help us.

14 September 2011

I was working at my desk that afternoon, when the phone rang.

It was Minister Vandeurzen's deputy head of cabinet.

"Am I disturbing you?" she asked. As if!

"I think that we have good news for you. Yesterday we received a phone call from the cabinet of the Minister of Justice. They have decided to accept the court ruling in your case." (One week later, the American Attorney General was due to visit his Belgian counterpart.)

Once more I could not believe it.

I thanked the woman on the other end of the line profusely, because that was the polite thing to do. Inside, however, I felt nothing.

It was a while after I'd hung up before this news sank in. For the first, but not the last time, I cried tears of relief and joy, but also of anger and fear.

I pulled myself together and phoned Jeff, who was in Stockholm for work. It was his birthday the next day.

"How's this for a birthday present —they're not going to appeal!"

Jeff was silent for a few moments. I could hear the sound of voices in the background. Then he spoke: "Sorry, I'm in a meeting. What? Did I hear you right?"

We were both overwhelmed for a moment by the heavy emotion as all that weight fell from our shoulders. "I love you and our daughters so much." "I do too."

That evening, I crept quietly into our daughters' room. They were sleeping peacefully beside each other in their little white beds. I stroked their faces and held their tiny hands.

*: name has been changed for reasons of privacy

Epilogue: An adult, open and inclusive adoption policy

Since its turbulent start, the story of Maya, Ella, Jeff and myself has been a happy one.

At the moment of finishing work on this book, our daughters have already become two amazing girls who will be going to their third year of kindergarten (school in Belgium starts around the age of 2,5 years). They are in different classes at school here in Brussels where they both make their own friends. Both girls are fluent in Dutch, French and English. They are like peas in a pod, however, their personalities are very different. They are both beautiful, intelligent, girls who are funny and eager to learn. Maya is very talkative and always full of energy. Ella is sensitive, empathic and a real cuddler. The four of us form a closely knit family.

I am still campaigning for a more adult, open and inclusive policy on adoption. This is one of the reasons why I wrote this book. In the past few years, I have spoken to politicians from every democratic party, to diplomats, to the civil servants who have helped us whenever possible, to adoptive parents and adopted children, to birth mothers, to people who I know very well and to total strangers in order to find guidelines that might form the basis of a Flemish adoption policy that would be worthy of such a title.

Much has already changed. There is a new Flemish Adoption Officer. The new decree, which came into effect in 2013, set up a Flemish Centre for Adoption (VCA) which has a more positive and proactive approach to foreign channels. In early 2014 the VCA confirmed an adoption collaboration with South Africa that is also open to LGBT couples.

DIA = the Inter-Country Adoption Service of the Ministry of Justice (also known as the Federal Central Authority for adoption (FCA), a term from the Hague Convention regulating inter-country adoption).
Stefaan De Clerck was Minister of Justice (2009-2011).

Flanders (the Dutch-speaking part of Belgium) had a Flemish adoption officer, who fell under the Flemish Ministry of Welfare, Public Health and Family. The adoption official was in charge of the VCA (formerly known as the Flemish Central Authority, but this has been known as the Flemish Centre for Adoption since 2013).
Jo Vandeurzen was the Flemish Minister for Welfare, Public Health and Family (Summer 2009-2014).

The Office of Children's Issues in Washington DC was, and still is, part of the American Department of Foreign Affairs, and champions the interests of US citizens who are minors abroad.
Hillary Clinton was Minister of Foreign Affairs for the US (2009-2012).

Published by
Boekenplan, Maastricht, Netherlands
www.boekenplan.nl
The future of publishing, today at Boekenplan

www.ingramcontent.com/pod-product-compliance
Lightning Source LLC
Chambersburg PA
CBHW030848270326
41928CB00008B/1278